GCSE AQA
Chemistry
The Workbook

This book is for anyone doing **GCSE AQA Chemistry**.

It's full of **tricky questions**... each one designed to make you **sweat** — because that's the only way you'll get any **better**.

There are questions to see **what facts** you know. There are questions to see how well you can **apply those facts**. And there are questions to see what you know about **how science works**.

It's also got some daft bits in to try and make the whole experience at least vaguely entertaining for you.

What CGP is all about

Our sole aim here at CGP is to produce the highest quality books — carefully written, immaculately presented and dangerously close to being funny.

Then we work our socks off to get them out to you — at the cheapest possible prices.

Contents

Chemistry 1a — Products from Rocks

Atoms and Elements 1
The Periodic Table 2
Compounds and Mixtures 3
Balancing Equations 5
Using Limestone 7
Properties of Metals 11
Metals from Rocks 13
The Reactivity Series 15
Making Metals More Useful 16
More About Metals 18
Fractional Distillation of Crude Oil 19
Properties and Uses of Crude Oil 20
Using Crude Oil as a Fuel 21
Environmental Problems 22
Mixed Questions — Chemistry 1a 25

Chemistry 1b — Oils, Earth and Atmosphere

Cracking Crude Oil 29
Alkenes and Ethanol 30
Using Alkenes to Make Polymers 31
Plant Oils and Emulsions 33
Extracting and Using Plant Oils 34
Using Plant Oils 36
Food Additives 37
Plate Tectonics 39
The Earth's Structure 41
The Evolution of the Atmosphere 43
Mixed Questions — Chemistry 1b 47

Chemistry 2(i) — Bonding and Reactions

Atoms 50
Elements, Compounds and Isotopes 51
The Periodic Table 52
Electron Shells 53
Ionic Bonding 55
Electron Shells and Ions 57
Covalent Bonding 58
Covalent Substances: Two Kinds 59
Metallic Structures 60
New Materials 62
Relative Formula Mass 64
Two Formula Mass Calculations 65
Calculating Masses in Reactions 66
The Mole 68
Atom Economy 70
Percentage Yield 71
Mixed Questions — Chemistry 2(i) 72

Chemistry 2(ii) — Rates of Reaction

Rates of Reaction 74
Measuring Rates of Reaction 75
Rate of Reaction Experiments 77
Collision Theory 81
Catalysts 82
Energy Transfer in Reactions 83
Reversible Reactions 85
The Haber Process 87
Mixed Questions — Chemistry 2(ii) 88

Chemistry 2(iii) — Using Ions in Solution

Acids and Alkalis 90
Acids Reacting with Metals 92
Oxides, Hydroxides and Ammonia 94
Making Salts 96
Electrolysis and the Half-Equations 98
Electrolysis of Salt Water 99
Purifying Copper by Electrolysis 101
Mixed Questions — Chemistry 2(iii) 102

Chemistry 3(i) — Elements, Acids and Water

History of the Periodic Table 104
The Modern Periodic Table 105
Group I — The Alkali Metals 107
Group VII — The Halogens 108
Transition Elements 109
Acids and Alkalis 111
Acids, Alkalis and Titration 112
Titration Calculations 113
Water 115
Solubility 117
Hard Water 119
Water Quality 121
Mixed Questions — Chemistry 3(i) 122

Chemistry 3(ii) — Energy and Chemical Tests

Energy 125
Energy and Fuels 126
Bond Energies 127
Energy and Food 129
Tests for Cations 130
Tests for Anions 132
Tests for Organic Compounds 133
Instrumental Methods 135
Identifying Unknown Substances 136
Mixed Questions — Chemistry 3(ii) 138

Answers 141

Published by Coordination Group Publications Ltd.

Editors:
Ellen Bowness, Sarah Hilton, Kate Houghton, Sharon Keeley, Kate Redmond,
Ami Snelling, Julie Wakeling.

From original material by:
Paddy Gannon

Contributors:
Michael Aicken, Antonio Angelosanto, Mike Dagless, Ian H. Davis, Max Fishel,
Rebecca Harvey, Munir Kawar, Lucy Muncaster, Andy Rankin, Sidney Stringer
Community School, Paul Warren.

ISBN: 978 1 84762 490 1

With thanks to Barrie Crowther and Glenn Rogers for the proofreading.
With thanks to Laura Jakubowski for the copyright research.

With thanks to East Midlands Aggregate Working Party/National Stone Centre for permission to reproduce the data used on page 8.

Groovy website: www.cgpbooks.co.uk

Printed by Elanders Hindson Ltd, Newcastle upon Tyne.
Jolly bits of clipart from CorelDRAW®

Based on the classic CGP style created by Richard Parsons.

Text, design, layout and original illustrations © Coordination Group Publications Ltd. 2010
All rights reserved.

Chemistry 1a — Products from Rocks

Atoms and Elements

Q1 a) Draw a diagram of a **helium atom**.

   b) Label each type of **particle** on your diagram.

Helium has 2 of each type of particle.

Q2 Look at these diagrams of substances. Circle the ones that contain only **one element**.

copper   oxygen   water   ethane

Q3 Many everyday substances, such as gold and aluminium, are **elements**. Other substances such as water and sugar are not.

Explain what this means in terms of the **atoms** in them.

....

....

Q4 Fill in the blanks to complete these sentences.

   a) The number of .... in an atom tells us which type of element it is.

   b) The nucleus of an atom consists of .... and ....

   c) Electrons are found in .... around the ....

   d) Hydrogen has the smallest atoms. A hydrogen atom contains only one .... and one ....

Chemistry 1a — Products from Rocks

The Periodic Table

Q1 Choose from these words to fill in the blanks.

left-hand   right-hand   horizontal   similar   different
vertical   metals   non-metals   transition

a) A group in the periodic table is a .... line of elements.

b) Most of the elements in the periodic table are ....

c) The elements between group II and group III are called .... metals.

d) Non-metals are on the .... side of the periodic table.

e) Elements in the same group have .... properties.

Q2 Argon is an extremely **unreactive** gas. Use the periodic table to give the names of two more gases that you would expect to have similar properties to argon.

1. ....
2. ....

Q3 Use the **periodic table** to complete the following table.

Element	Symbol	Reaction with magnesium	Formula of substance formed
Fluorine			MgF$_2$
	Cl	burns quickly	MgCl$_2$
Bromine			

Q4 Mendeleev (who **drew up** the periodic table) left gaps where he predicted undiscovered elements would fit. One of the gaps he left was **below silicon**. How did the **arrangement** of the periodic table help scientists know when they had found the missing element?

....
....
....

Chemistry 1a — Products from Rocks

Compounds and Mixtures

Q1 Seawater is a **mixture** of water and various dissolved substances, such as sodium chloride (table salt). **Water** is a **compound** of **hydrogen** and **oxygen**.

Are these statements true or false?

                                                                    True False

a) The substances in seawater are not chemically bonded to each other. ☐ ☐

b) Water can be separated into hydrogen and oxygen by boiling it. ☐ ☐

c) When seawater is heated until all the water evaporates, the only thing that is left behind is table salt. ☐ ☐

d) The formula for water is H_2O because it contains two hydrogen atoms joined to one oxygen atom. ☐ ☐

Q2 Choose from these words to fill in the blanks. Some words may be used more than once.

compounds   different   bonds   identical   separate   taking

electrons   elements

When atoms of different elements react they form bonds by giving away, taking or sharing .... The chemicals produced are called .... and are usually very difficult to .... using physical methods. The properties of compounds are .... from those of the elements used to make them. Mixtures are usually easier to .... because there are no chemical .... between their different parts.

Q3 Crude oil contains a lot of different substances. Most of them contain carbon joined to hydrogen and are called **hydrocarbons** (e.g. octane, C_8H_{18}, and pentane, C_5H_{12}). The majority of these hydrocarbons are **liquids**. To separate them the oil is **distilled**. Explain why **distillation** is a good way to **separate** these liquids.

....

....

Top Tips:
Compounds always contain two or more different elements **bonded together**. Mixtures also contain two or more elements and the particles in them can be compounds. The difference is that mixtures contain at least two sorts of particles that are **not chemically joined** together.

Chemistry 1a — Products from Rocks

Compounds and Mixtures

Q4 Andy puts some **magnesium metal** powder (which is a silver coloured powder) into a container of **oxygen** gas. Andy **heats** the contents of the container, allows them to cool and then describes what he can see in the container. Here are his results:

Appearance of powder	
Before heating	After heating
Silver coloured powder	White powder

a) Are magnesium and oxygen **elements**, **compounds** or **mixtures**?
....

b) At the end of the experiment is the powder a **mixture** or a **compound**?
....

c) What happens in the container to make the appearance of the contents change?
....

d) Write a **word equation** for the reaction that takes place in the container.
....

e) Would it be easier for Andy to use **physical methods** to separate the contents of the container **before** or **after** he heats them?
....

Q5 Circle the formula that contains the **most nitrogen** atoms.

NH_4Cl $(NH_4)_2CO_3$ N_2O_5 NO_2

$Al(NO_3)_3$ NH_3 NH_3NO_3

Top Tips: Sometimes you'll see formulas for chemicals that you've never heard of. Don't get stressed out — the same rules for identifying the elements that are in them apply to them all. So once you've got the hang of some simple ones like H_2O, you'll be able to do them all night long.

Chemistry 1a — Products from Rocks

Balancing Equations

Q1 Which of the following equations are **balanced** correctly?

		Correctly balanced	Incorrectly balanced
a)	$H_2 + Cl_2 \rightarrow 2HCl$	☐	☐
b)	$CuO + HCl \rightarrow CuCl_2 + H_2O$	☐	☐
c)	$N_2 + H_2 \rightarrow NH_3$	☐	☐
d)	$CuO + H_2 \rightarrow Cu + H_2O$	☐	☐
e)	$CaCO_3 \rightarrow CaO + CO_2$	☐	☐

Q2 Here is the equation for the formation of carbon **mon**oxide in a poorly ventilated gas fire. It is **not** balanced correctly.

$$C + O_2 \rightarrow CO$$

Circle the **correctly balanced** version of this equation.

$$C + O_2 \rightarrow CO_2$$

$$C + O_2 \rightarrow 2CO$$

$$2C + O_2 \rightarrow 2CO$$

Q3 In a book, this is the description of a reaction: "**methane** (CH_4) can be burnt in **oxygen** (O_2) to make **carbon dioxide** (CO_2) and **water** (H_2O)".

a) What are the **reactants** and the **products** in this reaction?

Reactants: .... Products: ....

b) Write the **word equation** for this reaction.

....

c) Write the **balanced symbol equation** for the reaction.

....

Don't forget the oxygen ends up in both products

Top Tips: The most important thing to remember with balancing equations is that you can't change the **little numbers** — if you do that then you'll change the substance into something completely different. Just take your time and work through everything logically.

Chemistry 1a — Products from Rocks

Balancing Equations

Q4 Write out the balanced **symbol** equations for the unbalanced picture equations below.

a) $2Na + Cl_2 \rightarrow 2NaCl$

b) $4Li + O_2 \rightarrow 2Li_2O$

c) $MgCO_3 + 2HCl \rightarrow MgCl_2 + H_2O + CO_2$

d) $2Li + 2H_2O \rightarrow 2LiOH + H_2$

Q5 Add **one** number to each of these equations so that they are **correctly balanced**.

a) $CuO + HBr \rightarrow CuBr_2 + H_2O$

b) $H_2 + Br_2 \rightarrow HBr$

c) $Mg + O_2 \rightarrow 2MgO$

d) $2NaOH + H_2SO_4 \rightarrow Na_2SO_4 + H_2O$

Q6 **Balance** these equations by adding in numbers.

a) $NaOH + AlBr_3 \rightarrow NaBr + Al(OH)_3$

b) $FeCl_2 + Cl_2 \rightarrow FeCl_3$

c) $N_2 + H_2 \rightarrow NH_3$

d) $Fe + O_2 \rightarrow Fe_2O_3$

e) $NH_3 + O_2 \rightarrow NO + H_2O$

$Fe_2O_3 + 3CO \rightarrow 2Fe + 3CO_2$

Chemistry 1a — Products from Rocks

Using Limestone

Q1 a) What is the **chemical name** for limestone?

....

b) What is the **chemical name** for quicklime?

....

Q2 Use the words below to fill the gaps in the passage.

sand   sodium carbonate   wood   concrete   clay   limestone
Heating powdered .... with clay in a kiln makes cement. When cement is mixed with water, gravel and sand it makes ...., which is a very common building material. Heating limestone with .... and .... makes glass.

Q3 **Carbonates** decompose to form two products.

a) Name the **two** products formed when limestone is heated.

1. ....

2. ....

b) What **solid** would you expect to be formed when **magnesium carbonate** is heated?

....

c) Write a **symbol equation** for the reaction that occurs when **copper carbonate** ($CuCO_3$) is heated.

....

Q4 The hills of Northern England are dotted with the remains of **lime kilns** where **limestone** ($CaCO_3$) was heated by farmers to make **quicklime** (CaO).

a) Write a word equation for the reaction that takes place in a lime kiln.

....

b) Quicklime reacts violently with water to make **slaked lime**, calcium hydroxide ($Ca(OH)_2$). Slaked lime is a weak alkali.

What do farmers use slaked lime for?

....

Chemistry 1a — Products from Rocks

Using Limestone

Q5 Heating metal carbonates is an example of **thermal decomposition**.

a) Explain what **thermal decomposition** means.

....

b) **Calcium oxide** and **calcium carbonate** are both white solids.
How could you tell the difference between them?

Think about what happens when you add quicklime to water.

....

c) How could you prove that carbon dioxide is produced when a metal carbonate is heated?

....

Q6 This passage is about **limestone extraction** in the Peak District National Park.
Read the extract and then answer the questions that follow.

The Peak District National Park covers about 1500 km^2 of land. Tourism is very important — a lot of people visit the area to enjoy the countryside. Limestone quarrying is also part of the local economy and there are 12 large quarries in the park. Some people aren't keen on all this — they say that quarrying is spoiling the natural beauty of the landscape, and discouraging tourists from visiting.

The limestone in the Peak District is very pure. It has been used locally in agriculture, and burned in lime kilns, for many years. When canals and railways were built in the area, limestone quarried in the park could be taken further afield, for use in industries elsewhere.
This continues today, and is another cause for concern — large lorries clog up narrow roads and disturb the peace and quiet in small villages.

A lot of limestone has been dug out of the Peak District. In 1990, 8.5 million tonnes of limestone were quarried from the Peak District National Park — more than five times as much as in 1951. This limestone is used in several different industries (the figures below are for 1989).

Use	Percentage
Aggregate (for road-building etc.)	55.8%
Cement	23%
Chemicals	17%
Iron and steel	4%
Agriculture	0.2%

Chemistry 1a — Products from Rocks

Using Limestone

a) What makes the **limestone** in the Peak District particularly useful?
....

b) Approximately how many tonnes of limestone were quarried in 1951?
....

c) Describe one way in which limestone has been used locally in the Peak District.
....

d) State **three problems** that are caused by quarrying limestone in the Peak District.

   1. ....

   2. ....

   3. ....

e) i) How was limestone originally **transported away** from the Peak District?
   ....

   ii) How is limestone **transported** today?
   ....

f) Do you think that the person who wrote the article is in favour of quarrying or against it? Explain the reasons for your answer.
   ....
   ....

g) Complete this table showing the amount of limestone quarried from the Peak District in 1989.

Use	Percentage	Total amount quarried in tonnes
Aggregate (for road-building etc.)	55.8%	
Cement	23%	
Chemicals	17%	
Iron and steel	4%	
Agriculture	0.2%	

Chemistry 1a — Products from Rocks

Using Limestone

Q7 Many of the products used to build houses are made with limestone. Circle the materials that have **no** connection to limestone.

glass   paint   bricks   cement   granite   concrete

Q8 In Norway **powdered limestone** is added to lakes that have been damaged by acid rain.

　a) Name the process that takes place when the powdered limestone reacts with the acid in the lake.

　　..

　b) Explain why powdered limestone is also used in the chimneys at power stations.

　　..

　　..

Q9 Limestone is a useful rock but **quarrying** it causes some **problems**.

　a) Describe two problems that quarrying limestone can cause.

　　1. ....

　　2. ....

　b) Explain how limestone quarries may benefit the local community.

　　..

　　..

Q10 What are the **advantages** of using **concrete** instead of these traditional building materials?

　a) Wood: ....

　b) Metals: ....

　c) Bricks: ....

Chemistry 1a — Products from Rocks

Properties of Metals

Q1 Most **metals** that are used to make everyday objects are found in the **central section** of the periodic table.

a) What name is given to this group of metals?

....

b) Why could metals from this group be used to make electrical wires?

....

Q2 This table shows some of the **properties** of four different **metals**.

Metal	Heat conduction	Cost	Resistance to corrosion	Strength
1	average	high	excellent	good
2	average	medium	good	excellent
3	excellent	low	good	good
4	low	high	average	poor

Use the information in the table to choose which metal would be **best** for making each of the following:

a) Saucepan bases ....

b) Car bodies ....

c) A statue to be placed in a town centre ....

Think about how long a statue would have to last for.

Q3 What **properties** would you look for if you were asked to choose a **metal** suitable for making knives and forks?

....

....

....

Top Tips: Remember most elements are metals and most metals have similar properties. But don't be a fool and think they're all identical — there are lots of little differences which make them useful for different things. Some metals are pretty weird, for example mercury is liquid at room temperature, which means it's not ideal for making cars.

Chemistry 1a — Products from Rocks

Properties of Metals

Q4 In an experiment some identically sized rods of different materials (A, B, C and D) were **heated** at one end and **temperature sensors** were connected to the other ends. The results are shown in the graph.

a) Which two rods do you think were made from metals?

....

b) Which of the metals was the best conductor of heat and how can you tell?

....

Q5 All metals have a similar structure. This explains why many of them have similar properties.

a) Draw a labelled diagram of a typical metal structure.

b) What is unusual about the electrons in a metal?

Think about the reasons why metals are good conductors.

....

Q6 Imagine that a space probe has brought a sample of a new element back from Mars. Scientists think that the element is a **metal**, but they aren't certain. Give **three properties** they could look for to provide evidence that the element is a **metal**.

1. ....

2. ....

3. ....

Top Tips: Ever wondered why we don't make bridges out of platinum? Cost is a big factor in the use of metals, so even if a metal is perfect for a job it might not be used because it's too expensive. The cheapest metals are the ones that are both common and easy to extract from their ores.

Chemistry 1a — Products from Rocks

Metals from Rocks

Q1 **Copper** is used to make electrical wires.

a) Copper can be extracted from its ore by reduction with carbon.
Why **can't** copper produced in this way be used for electrical wires?

....

b) How is copper that **is** suitable for making electrical wires produced?

....

c) Give another **common use** of copper.

....

Q2 Copper objects such as old pipes can be **recycled**.
Give **two** reasons why it is important to recycle copper.

1. ....

2. ....

Q3 The following extract is taken from a press release from a scientific research company.
Read the extract and then answer the questions below.

> *Here at Copperextra we are very excited about our latest developments.*
>
> *Within six months we expect to be extracting pure copper from material that would usually be wasted.*
>
> *We are also making interesting developments in using bacteria for extraction. Using the latest genetic modification techniques we have developed a new strain of bacteria that can separate copper from copper sulfide at twice the speed of unmodified bacteria. In the future it should also be possible to use this technology to extract a range of other metals.*

a) Why do you think the company is keen to develop a way of extracting copper from waste material?

....

....

b) Explain why using bacteria to extract copper from ores is more environmentally friendly than electrolysis.

....

....

Chemistry 1a — Products from Rocks

Metals from Rocks

Q4 This table shows some common **metal ores** and their formulas.

Ore	Formula
Haematite	Fe_2O_3
Magnetite	Fe_3O_4
Pyrites	FeS_2
Galena	PbS
Bauxite	Al_2O_3

Name the two elements that are commonly bonded to metals in ores.

....

Q5 **Gold** is often extracted from ores that contain very **small** percentages of the metal, but iron is only extracted from ores with a **large** percentage of the metal. Explain why.

....

....

Q6 New mines always have **social**, **economic** and **environmental** consequences. Complete this table to show the effects that a new mine can have.

Social	Economic	Environmental
Services, e.g. healthcare may be improved because of influx of people.		Pollution from traffic.

Remember to include both positive and negative effects.

Top Tips: Remember that metals are finite resources — there's a set amount on Earth and once we've extracted them all there won't be any more. We need to be able to get metals out of low-grade ores (ones that only contain small amounts of metal) to get enough to go round.

Chemistry 1a — Products from Rocks

The Reactivity Series

Q1 If zinc is heated with copper oxide this reaction happens:

zinc + copper oxide → copper + zinc oxide

a) Why does this reaction take place? ....

b) Would it be possible to produce zinc oxide by reacting zinc with aluminium oxide? ....

Explain your answer. ....

Q2 One of the first metals to be extracted from its ore was **copper**. The discovery may have happened when someone accidentally dropped some copper ore into a wood fire. When the ashes were cleared away some copper was left.

a) What was the source of carbon in the fire?

....

b) Why do you think that copper was one of the first metals to be extracted from its ore?

....

c) Many metals, like potassium and magnesium, were not discovered until the early 1800s. What had to be developed before they could be extracted?

How are they extracted?

....

Q3 Fill in the blanks in this passage:

.... can be used to extract metals that are .... it in the reactivity series. Oxygen is removed from the metal oxide in a process called .... Other metals have to be extracted using .... because they are .... reactive.

Q4 Imagine that four new metals, **antium**, **bodium**, **candium** and **dekium** have recently been discovered. Bodium displaces antium but not candium or dekium. Dekium displaces all the others. Put the new metals into their order of reactivity, from the most to the least reactive.

....

Top Tips: Stuff on the reactivity series isn't easy, so don't worry too much if you found these questions difficult. You don't need to learn the reactivity series off by heart, so spend plenty of time making sure that you understand reduction, electrolysis and displacement reactions.

Chemistry 1a — Products from Rocks

Making Metals More Useful

Q1 Most iron is made into the alloy **steel**.

a) Write a definition of the term '**alloy**'.

....

....

b) How is **iron** turned into **steel**?

....

....

Tonight Matthew, I'm going to be... steel.

Q2 Draw lines to connect the correct phrases in each column. One has been done for you.

Metal / Alloy	What has been added	Use
low-carbon steel	nothing	blades for tools
iron from a blast furnace	chromium	cutlery
high-carbon steel	0.1% carbon	car bodies
stainless steel	1.5% carbon	ornamental railings

(line drawn from "iron from a blast furnace" to "nothing" to "ornamental railings")

Q3 Complete the following sentences using the metals below.

gold   copper   silver   nickel   titanium

a) Bronze is an alloy that contains ....

b) Cupronickel, which is used in 'silver' coins, contains copper and ....

c) To make gold hard enough for jewellery it is mixed with metals such as ....

Chemistry 1a — Products from Rocks

Making Metals More Useful

Q4 Draw a diagram showing the structure of **iron**. Annotate your diagram to explain why iron and other metals can be **bent** and **shaped** without breaking.

Q5 24-carat gold is **pure** gold. 9-carat gold contains **9 parts** gold to 15 parts other metals. 9-carat gold is **harder** and **cheaper** than 24-carat gold.

   a) What percentage of 9-carat gold is actually gold?

   ....

   b) Why is 9-carat gold harder than pure gold?

   ....

   ....

Q6 Recently, scientists have been developing **smart alloys** with **shape memory** properties.

   a) Give an example of a use for smart alloys.

   ....

   b) What **advantages** do smart alloys have over ordinary metals?

   ....

   ....

   Smart Alloy of the Month Award
   Presented to: Nitinol
   Presented by: CGP

   c) Give **two disadvantages** of using smart alloys.

   ....

   ....

Top Tips: As you must know by now, metals have lots of pretty useful properties, but they can be made even more useful by being mixed together to make alloys. Smart alloys are great for making those bendy glasses that don't break when you sit on them.

Chemistry 1a — Products from Rocks

More About Metals

Q1 a) **Aluminium** and **titanium** are similar in some ways but different in others.
Complete this table to compare the properties of **aluminium** with those of **titanium**.

Property	Aluminium	Titanium
Density	low	low
Reactivity		
Strength		
Corrosion resistance	high	high
Cost		

b) What **properties** of **titanium** make it particularly useful for making **artificial hip joints**?

....

Q2 **Aluminium** and **titanium** are both described as **corrosion resistant**.
If you put a small piece of each metal into a beaker of dilute, hot **hydrochloric acid** nothing will happen for several minutes. Then the **aluminium** will start to bubble quickly and dissolve. The **titanium** will not change. Explain why the two metals behave like this.

....

....

....

Q3 Wherever possible, every scrap of gold is **recycled**. We also recycle **aluminium** as much as possible, even though it is the most common metal in the Earth's crust. Explain the reasons why we **recycle** these two metals.

....

....

....

Top Tips: Well, I hope you've had fun on this metals extravaganza. The good news is that none of this is too complicated — just make sure you've learnt the properties of the everyday metals like iron, aluminium and titanium and why they're so useful.

Chemistry 1a — Products from Rocks

Fractional Distillation of Crude Oil

Q1 Circle the correct words to complete these sentences.

a) Crude oil is a **mixture** / **compound** of different molecules.

b) The molecules in crude oil **are** / **aren't** chemically bonded to each other.

c) If crude oil were heated the **first** / **last** thing to boil off would be bitumen.

d) Diesel has **larger** / **smaller** molecules than petrol.

Q2 Label this diagram of a **fractionating column** to show where these substances can be collected.

petrol   kerosene   diesel   oil   bitumen

These are in order of smallest to largest molecules from left to right.

Q3 What is the connection between the **size** of the **molecules** in crude oil and their **condensing** (or **boiling**) points?

....

....

Q4 The fractional distillation of crude oil is described as a **continuous process**. What does this mean?

....

....

Chemistry 1a — Products from Rocks

Properties and Uses of Crude Oil

Q1 Crude oil is a mixture of **hydrocarbons**. These **hydrocarbons** are mostly **alkanes**.

a) Draw the structures of the first four **alkanes** and name each alkane you have drawn.

b) Which of the alkanes you have drawn would you expect to have the highest boiling point?

....

Q2 There are some basic **trends** in the way that **alkanes** behave. Circle the correct words to complete these sentences.

a) The longer the alkane molecule the **more / less** viscous (gloopy) it is.

b) The shorter the alkane molecule the **more / less** volatile it is.

c) A very volatile liquid is one with a **low / high** boiling point.

Q3 a) What is the **general formula** for **alkanes**?

If you can't remember it you can work it out by looking at the diagrams you have drawn at the top of the page.

....

b) **Eicosane** is a hydrocarbon that can be used to make candles. Each molecule of eicosane contains **20 carbon** atoms. What is the **chemical formula** for eicosane?

....

Q4 Each hydrocarbon molecule in engine oil has a **long** string of carbon atoms.

a) Explain why this type of oil is good for using as a **lubricant** in an engine.

....

b) Engines get very **hot** when they are in use. Why would oil molecules with **short** carbon chains be unsuitable for use as lubricants?

....

....

Chemistry 1a — Products from Rocks

Using Crude Oil as a Fuel

Q1 Crude oil **fractions** are often used as **fuels**.

Give **four** examples of fuels that are made from crude oil.

Remember fuels aren't just used in vehicles.

....

Q2 As crude oil is a **non-renewable** resource people are keen to find **alternative** energy sources. Suggest a problem with each of these ways of using alternative fuels.

a) **Solar** energy for cars: ....

b) **Wind** energy to power an oven: ....

c) **Nuclear** energy for buses: ....

Q3 Using oil products as fuels causes some **environmental** problems.
Explain the environmental problems that are associated with each of the following:

a) **Transporting** crude oil across the sea in tankers.

....

b) **Burning** oil products to release the energy they contain.

....

Q4 Forty years ago some scientists predicted that there would be no oil left by the year 2000, but obviously they were **wrong**. One reason is that modern engines are more **efficient** than ones in the past, so they use less fuel. Give two other reasons why the scientists' prediction was wrong.

....

....

Q5 Write a short paragraph summarising why crude oil is the most **common source** of fuel even though **alternatives** are available.

....

....

....

Chemistry 1a — Products from Rocks

Environmental Problems

Q1 Draw lines to link the correct parts of these sentences.

The main cause of acid rain is — acid rain.

Acid rain kills trees and — sulfuric acid.

Limestone buildings and statues are affected by — acidifies lakes.

In clouds sulfur dioxide reacts with water to make — sulfur dioxide.

Q2 Give **three** ways that the amount of **acid rain** can be reduced.

....

....

....

Q3 a) Write a word equation for completely **burning** a **hydrocarbon** in the open air.

....

b) Write **balanced symbol equations** for completely burning these alkanes in open air:

i) Methane: ....

ii) Propane: ....

Q4 **Exhaust** fumes from cars and lorries often contain **carbon monoxide** and **carbon particles**.

a) Why are they more likely to be formed in **engines** than if the fuel was burnt in the open air?

....

b) Why is carbon monoxide **dangerous**?

....

Top Tips: The best way to prevent acid rain damage is to reduce the amount of sulfur dioxide that we release into the atmosphere. When acid rain does fall there are some ways of reducing the amount of damage it causes, such as adding powdered limestone to affected lakes.

Chemistry 1a — Products from Rocks

Environmental Problems

Q5 Look at the graph and then answer the questions below.

a) Describe the **trend** shown by the graph.

....

b) What is the main cause of this trend?

....

c) What effect do scientists believe the trend shown in the graph is having on the Earth's average temperature?

....

Q6 **Hydrogen** is often talked about as the 'fuel of the future'.

a) What is the **only product** produced when **hydrogen** is burned?

....

b) Why is it better for the **environment** if we burn hydrogen rather than petrol?

....

c) Currently, most of the vehicles that can use hydrogen as a fuel are demonstration vehicles that are being developed by scientists. Explain the problems that will have to be overcome before the public will be able to use hydrogen-powered vehicles on a large scale.

....

....

....

Think about storage of hydrogen and the costs involved.

Top Tips: Scientists are constantly looking at the ways people are damaging the environment and trying to come up with ways of reducing the damage. But different scientists have different opinions on issues like global warming and they don't all agree about what should be done.

Chemistry 1a — Products from Rocks

Environmental Problems

Q7 In Brazil **ethanol** produced by **fermenting** sugar cane is a popular fuel for vehicles. The ethanol is mixed with **petrol** before it is used.

a) What products are produced when **ethanol** (C_2H_5OH) is completely burnt?

....

b) Why is ethanol made in this way a **carbon neutral** fuel?

....

Q8 **Biogas** is a mixture of **methane** (CH_4) and **carbon dioxide**. It is produced by microorganisms digesting waste material.

a) What products are formed when **biogas** is burnt?

....

b) What would be the main problem with using a **biogas generator** in Iceland?

....

Q9 Scientists are working hard to develop new **technologies** that are **environmentally friendly**.

a) Summarise the developments in technology in these areas that are helping to reduce environmental damage:

i) Sulfur emissions from power stations ....

....

ii) Carbon dioxide emissions from vehicles ....

....

b) List some ways that people can alter their lifestyles so that they cause less environmental damage.

....

....

c) Do you think it is solely the responsibility of scientists to find ways of reducing environmental damage or should people be prepared to change their lifestyles too? Explain your answer.

....

....

....

Mixed Questions — Chemistry 1a

Q1 Metals make up about 80% of all the elements in the periodic table.

a) Shade the area where **metals** are found on this periodic table:

b) Read each of the following statements about metals. If the statement is true, tick the box.
- ☐ Metals are generally strong but also malleable.
- ☐ Metals are shiny when freshly cut or polished.
- ☐ Metal atoms are held together with ionic bonds.
- ☐ Generally, metals have low melting and boiling points.
- ☐ Properties of a metal can be altered by mixing it with another metal to form an alloy.

c) Metals are good electrical conductors. Explain why this is the case.
You should use ideas about **structure** and **bonding** in your answer.

....

....

....

d) Look at the information in the table below. R, S, T and U are all metals.
Explain in detail which material would be most suitable to build an **aeroplane body**.

Material	Strength	Cost (£)	Density (g/cm³)	Melting Point (°C)
R	High	100	3	1000
S	Medium	90	5	150
T	High	450	8	1200
U	Low	200	11	1070

....

....

....

Q2 The extraction, transportation and processing of crude oil is a major industry.

a) Name one product of the crude oil industry, other than a fuel.

....

b) Name one problem associated with the **transportation** of crude oil.

....

Chemistry 1a — Products from Rocks

Mixed Questions — Chemistry 1a

Q3 The metals **aluminium**, **copper** and **iron** can be extracted from their **ores**.

a) Metal ores are often described as 'finite resources'. Explain the term '**finite resource**'.

   ....

b) The table shows the **reactivity series** of metals and **dates of discovery**.

   i) What pattern can be seen in the data?

   ....

   ....

   ii) Suggest an explanation for this.

   ....

   ....

   ....

metal	discovery	
potassium	AD 1807	most reactive ↑
sodium	AD 1807	
calcium	AD 1808	
magnesium	AD 1755	
aluminium	AD 1825	
carbon		
zinc	about AD 1400	
iron	about 2500 BC	
tin	about 2000 BC	
lead	about 3500 BC	
hydrogen		
copper	about 4200 BC	
silver	about 4000 BC	
gold	about 6000 BC	
platinum	before 1500 BC	↓ least reactive

c) Complete the following table by adding the **name** of a common ore of each metal and its **formula**.

metal	name of ore	chemical formula of ore
iron	haematite	
aluminium		
copper		

d) i) Complete the word equation for the reduction of iron ore with carbon monoxide.

   iron(III) oxide + ... → **iron** + ...

   ii) Write a **balanced symbol equation** for this reaction. (The formula of iron(III) oxide is Fe_2O_3.)

   ....

e) Copper metal can be extracted from its ore by **reduction** using carbon then purified by **electrolysis**.

   i) Explain why electrolysis is used to produce copper metal for **electrical wiring**.

   ....

   ii) Give **two** physical properties of copper that make it suitable for use in **electrical wiring**.

   1. ....

   2. ....

f) One of the most common elements present in the Earth's crust is aluminium.
   Explain why aluminium metal can only be extracted using **electrolysis**.

   ....

   ....

Chemistry 1a — Products from Rocks

Mixed Questions — Chemistry 1a

Q4 **Petrol** and **diesel** are two commonly used fuels for cars.

a) Diesel has longer molecules than petrol.
List **four** differences you would expect in physical properties between petrol and diesel.

1. ....
2. ....
3. ....
4. ....

b) **Ethanol** is an alternative fuel to petrol and diesel.

i) How can ethanol be produced? ....

ii) Why is ethanol a more environmentally friendly fuel?

....

Q5 **Lubricating oils** in car engines keep moving metal surfaces apart. Viscous oils do this better than runny oils, but if they're too viscous they don't lubricate the moving parts properly.

The following experiment was set up to find which of two oils was the more viscous.
The time taken for each oil to run through the burette was noted at two temperatures.

Burette	Temperature (°C)	Time for 50 cm³ of oil to flow through (s)
1	20	90
2	40	53
3	20	64
4	40	28

Use the table of results to answer the following questions:

a) Which oil is **more viscous** at 20 °C? ....

b) Temperatures in an engine are much higher than 40 °C.
What will happen to the viscosity of these oils at engine temperature?

....

c) How could you **improve** the experiment to find out which oil would be more viscous when used in an engine?

....

d) Which oil would you expect to be tapped off closer to the top of a fractionating column?

....

Chemistry 1a — Products from Rocks

Mixed Questions — Chemistry 1a

Q6 **Calcium carbonate** ($CaCO_3$), in the form of the rock **limestone**, is one of the most important raw materials for the chemical and construction industries.

a) Limestone can be processed to form **slaked lime**.

i) Complete the flow diagram.

common name	limestone	+ HEAT (A) →	calcium oxide	+ WATER (B) →	slaked lime
chemical name	calcium carbonate		calcium oxide		
formula	$CaCO_3$		CaO		

ii) Write a balanced symbol equation for reaction A.

.... → .... + ...

iii) Give one use of slaked lime.

....

b) Limestone can be processed to form useful building materials. Complete the flow diagram.

Limestone → (heat with clay) → [ ] → (add sand, water and gravel) → [ ]

Limestone → (heat with sand and sodium carbonate) → [ ]

c) Give **two** reasons why limestone is more likely to be used as a building material than **wood**.

1. ....

2. ....

d) Limestone is also used in the manufacture of **glass**.

i) Name the other two main ingredients of glass.

....

ii) By what simple process are these ingredients turned into glass?

....

e) The limestone of the Houses of Parliament is crumbling away.

What is causing the damage to the limestone and how?

....

Chemistry 1a — Products from Rocks

Chemistry 1b — Oils, Earth and Atmosphere

Cracking Crude Oil

Q1 Fill in the gaps with the words below.

| high | shorter | long | catalyst | cracking | diesel | molecules | petrol |

There is more need for .... chain fractions of crude oil such as .... than for longer chains such as ....

Heating .... hydrocarbon molecules to .... temperatures with a .... breaks them down into smaller .... This is called ....

Q2 Diesel is **cracked** to produce products that are more in demand.

a) Suggest three useful substances that are produced when diesel is cracked.

....

b) Write down a reason why long hydrocarbons do not make good fuels.

....

c) What type of reaction is cracking? ....

Q3 After cracking both **alkenes** and **alkanes** are present.

a) Bromine water is used to test whether a substance is an alkane or alkene. Alkenes decolourise bromine water, but alkanes don't.

Which of the following would decolourise bromine water?

☐ propane   ☐ ethane   ☐ ethene

Alkanes end with -ane, alkenes end with -ene.

b) Put the steps of the cracking process in the correct order by writing numbers in the boxes.

☐ The vapour is passed over a catalyst at a high temperature.
☐ The long-chain molecules are heated.
☐ The molecules are cracked on the surface of the catalyst.
☐ They are vaporised (turned into a gas).

Q4 Change this diagram into a **word equation** and a **symbol equation**.

kerosene →(CRACKING)→ octane + ethene

a) Word equation: .... → .... + ...

b) Symbol equation: .... → .... + ...

Alkenes and Ethanol

Q1 Complete this table showing the molecular and displayed formulas of some alkenes.

Alkene	Formula	Displayed formula
Ethene	a)	b)
c)	C_3H_6	d)
Butene	C_4H_8	e)

There are 2 different forms of butene — draw both.

Q2 The general formula for alkenes is C_nH_{2n}. Use it to write down the formulas of these alkenes.

a) pentene (5 carbons) ....   b) hexene (6 carbons) ....

c) octene (8 carbons) ....   d) dodecene (12 carbons) ....

Q3 True or false?

                                                                        True False

a) Alkenes have double bonds between the hydrogen atoms. ☐ ☐

b) Alkenes are unsaturated. ☐ ☐

c) Alkenes are not very useful. ☐ ☐

d) Ethene has two carbon atoms. ☐ ☐

Q4 There are two ways of making ethanol:

    A Sugar → ethanol + carbon dioxide   B Ethene + steam → ethanol

a) Which of the word equations describes making ethanol by **fermentation**? ....

b) Ethanol can be used as a fuel. In some countries the fermentation method is often used to produce it. Give two reasons why this method is chosen.

1. ....

2. ....

c) Give a disadvantage of the fermentation method.

....

d) What conditions are needed to make ethanol from ethene and steam?

....

....

Chemistry 1b — Oils, Earth and Atmosphere

Using Alkenes to Make Polymers

Q1 Tick the box next to the **true** statement below.

☐ The monomer of poly(ethene) is ethene.

☐ The polymer of poly(ethene) is ethane.

☐ The monomer of poly(ethene) is ethane.

Q2 **Low density poly(ethene)** and **high density poly(ethene)** are both made from the same monomers, but have very different properties.

a) Explain what causes the different properties.

....

....

b) Poly(styrene) and poly(propene) have different properties. Why is this likely to be?

....

....

Q3 Most polymers are **not** biodegradable.

Biodegradable means that something can rot.

a) What problems does this cause for the environment?

....

....

b) How can you minimise this environmental problem when using objects made from polymers?

....

....

c) Things are often made from plastics because they are cheap. Why might this change in the future?

....

....

Chemistry 1b — Oils, Earth and Atmosphere

Using Alkenes to Make Polymers

Q4 The equation below shows the polymerisation of ethene to form **poly(ethene)**.

$$n \begin{pmatrix} H & H \\ | & | \\ C = C \\ | & | \\ H & H \end{pmatrix} \longrightarrow \begin{pmatrix} H & H \\ | & | \\ -C - C- \\ | & | \\ H & H \end{pmatrix}_n$$

many ethene molecules → poly(ethene)

Draw a similar equation below to show the polymerisation of propene (C_3H_6).

It's easier if you think of propene as

$$\begin{matrix} H & & H \\ & C=C & \\ H & & CH_3 \end{matrix}$$

Q5 Fractional distillation of crude oil produces useful fractions and not-so-useful fractions. The not-so-useful ones are **cracked** to form alkenes. Alkenes can be **polymerised** to make plastics.

Write down the differences between cracking and polymerisation.

....

....

....

Q6 Harvey makes two samples of slime by mixing poly(ethenol) with sodium tetraborate. The slime samples are made with two **different concentrations** of sodium tetraborate solution.

Harvey places a ball of each slime sample in the centre of a circular disc and times how long it takes for the samples to flow to the outside of the disc. His results are shown below.

Sample	Time (seconds)
A	14
B	31

a) Which slime sample was made from the strongest solution of sodium tetraborate? Explain your answer.

....

....

b) Suggest one thing that Harvey should have kept the same to make it a fair test.

....

Top Tips: It's amazingly easy to name polymers. You just take the name of the monomer (the little molecules that are joined together) stick it in brackets, and write the word 'poly' in front of it. And Bob's your uncle (except if his name's Mike or anything else that's not Bob).

Chemistry 1b — Oils, Earth and Atmosphere

Plant Oils and Emulsions

Q1 Oil can be extracted from some **fruits** and **seeds**.

a) Name two fruits and two seeds which are good sources of oil.

Fruits: .... and ....

Seeds: .... and ....

b) Give two uses of plant oils. ....

c) Why is the use of **high pressure** an important part of the oil extraction process?

....

d) **Centrifugation** is the high speed spinning of a material. Why is it often used in oil extraction?

....

Q2 Each of these sentences has an error. Write out a **correct version** of each sentence.

a) Vegetable oils provide loads of energy, but are not nutritious.

....

b) Emulsions are always formed from oil suspended in water.

....

c) The thicker an emulsion, the less oil it contains.

....

d) Emulsions can be combined with air, but it makes them runnier.

....

Air is whipped into cream to make a topping for a trifle.

e) Emulsions are only found in foods.

....

Q3 Milk and cream are both **oil-in-water emulsions**.
They have different properties because of their different compositions.

In the boxes below draw diagrams to show the composition of the oil-in-water emulsions **milk**, **single cream** and **double cream**.

Milk	Single cream	Double cream

Chemistry 1b — Oils, Earth and Atmosphere

Extracting and Using Plant Oils

Q1 Vegetable oils can be turned into fuels.

a) Name two vegetable oils that can be turned into fuels.

.... and ....

b) Why are vegetable oils suitable for processing into fuels?

....

Q2 Biodiesel is a fuel made from vegetable oil.
A litre of biodiesel contains **90%** of the energy found in a litre of normal diesel.

Normal diesel contains 37 megajoules (37 000 000 J) of energy per litre.
How much energy does a litre of biodiesel contain?

....

Q3 Biodiesel is more environmentally friendly than normal diesel or petrol.
However, it is unlikely to replace them in the near future.

a) Give three reasons why biodiesel is more environmentally friendly than petrol or normal diesel.

1. ....

2. ....

3. ....

b) Explain why biodiesel is unlikely to replace petrol or normal diesel in the near future.

....

c) Give two advantages that biodiesel has over other "green" car fuels such as biogas.

1. ....

2. ....

Q4 Biodiesel is said to be "**carbon neutral**".

a) Explain why this is.

....

....

b) Why is normal diesel not carbon neutral?

....

....

Chemistry 1b — Oils, Earth and Atmosphere

Extracting and Using Plant Oils

Q5 Read this passage and answer the questions below.

> Biodiesel is a liquid fuel which can be made from vegetable oils. It's renewable, and can be used instead of ordinary diesel in cars and lorries. It can also be blended with normal diesel — this is common in some countries, such as France. You don't have to modify your car's engine to use biodiesel.
>
> Biodiesel has several advantages. Producing and using it releases 80% less carbon dioxide overall than producing and using fossil-fuel diesel. So if we want to do something about climate change, using biodiesel would be a good start. Biodiesel is also less harmful if it's accidentally spilled, because it's readily biodegradable.
>
> In the UK, we make most of our biodiesel from recycled cooking oils. But we don't make very much yet — you can only buy it from about 100 filling stations. The Government has been making some effort to encourage us to use more biodiesel. There's one major problem — it's about twice as expensive to make as ordinary diesel.
>
> Most of the price you pay for petrol or diesel is not the cost of the fuel — it's tax, which goes straight to the Government. Over the last decade, the Government has increased fuel taxes, making petrol and diesel more expensive to buy. Part of the reason they've done this is to try to put us off buying them — because burning fossil fuels releases harmful pollutants and contributes to climate change.
>
> So, to make biodiesel cheaper, in 2002, the Government cut the tax rate on it. The tax on biodiesel is now 20p/litre less than it is on normal diesel. This makes biodiesel a similar price to normal diesel. If the Government cuts the tax even further, then more people would be keen to use biodiesel, and more filling stations would start to sell it.

a) In the UK, what do we produce most of our biodiesel from at present?

....

b) What would the environmental impact be if biodiesel was more widely used?

....

....

c) What has the Government done to encourage people to switch from normal diesel to biodiesel?

....

....

d) If lots more people start buying biodiesel instead of normal diesel, what problem is this likely to cause for the Government?

....

....

e) "I don't want to change to biodiesel. I don't want all the hassle of getting my car modified, and biodiesel costs more. It's just another way for the Government to get money off the taxpayers."

Write a response to this using information from the passage above.

....

....

Chemistry 1b — Oils, Earth and Atmosphere

Using Plant Oils

Q1 Ben and Martin both planned an experiment to identify saturated and unsaturated oils.

Ben's Method
1. Put some oil in a test tube.
2. Add some bromine water.
3. Shake vigorously.
4. Repeat for next oil.
5. When all the oils are done, write down the results.

Martin's Method
1. Put 2 ml of oil into a test tube.
2. Label the test tube with the name of the oil sample.
3. Add 5 drops of bromine water.
4. Record any colour change.
5. Repeat for each oil.

Whose experimental method is better? Give reasons for your answer.

....

....

Q2 Match each label below to a fatty acid structure.

Saturated animal fat

Polyunsaturated grape seed oil

Monounsaturated olive oil

Q3 Margarine is usually made from partially hydrogenated vegetable oil.

a) Describe the process of hydrogenation.

....

....

b) How does hydrogenation affect the melting points of vegetable oils?

....

Q4 Some types of fats are considered bad for your heart.

a) Explain why saturated fats are bad for your heart.

....

....

b) Partially hydrogenated vegetable oil contains **trans fats**. What effect do these have on the blood?

....

Chemistry 1b — Oils, Earth and Atmosphere

Food Additives

Q1 Food colourings are usually made up of several different dyes. These can be separated out.

a) What is the name of the **separation** technique that allows us to examine the dyes used in foods?

....

b) Which dye is **more soluble**, A or B? ....

c) Which would travel more slowly, a **more soluble** or a **less soluble** dye?

....

Q2 Fill in the gaps in the passage using the words below. Use each word only once.

| additives | compounds | appearance | ingredients | salt | approved |
| longer | chemical | preserve | taste | E-numbers | sodium sorbate |

Nowadays there are a variety of ways to .... food, such as refrigeration, canning or pickling. One of the biggest advances has come through the use of ....

Using .... to preserve food is not a new idea. For hundreds of years people have been using .... to keep food fresh for .... Scientists have used this basic idea to develop a number of different additives that not only preserve food, but can alter other characteristics of foods, such as the texture, the .... or the ....

Most additives used in the UK have .... For example, the preservative .... is E201. These are chemical compounds which have been .... for use in Europe. The additives must be listed in the .... on the packaging.

Top Tips: Additives with E-numbers aren't always the evil things you might be led to believe they are. Take E300 for instance — it's ascorbic acid and stops food going off as quickly. It sounds very unnatural and you might think that it's bound to be bad for you. But it's actually just vitamin C.

Chemistry 1b — Oils, Earth and Atmosphere

Food Additives

Q3 Jacob did a chromatography experiment and got the following results.

a) Write a brief method for this experiment, describing what Jacob would have done.

Colour of Sweet	Distance Travelled by Dye (mm)		
Brown	10	17	18
Red	18		
Green	10	17	
Orange	10	18	26
Blue	5	17	

....

....

....

....

....

b) How many dyes do the results indicate that the blue sweet contains? ....

c) Which sweet might contain the same mix of dyes as the red and green sweets together? Give a reason for your answer.

....

....

Q4 "I try to avoid eating all additives. I don't want to put those unnatural chemicals into my body." Write a response to this statement using your knowledge about additives.

....

....

....

Q5 Use the ingredients list from a bottle of orange squash to answer the questions below.

Orange Squash
Water
Comminuted orange from concentrate (10%)
Citric acid
Acidity regulator (sodium citrate)
Flavourings
Sweeteners (aspartame, sodium saccharin)
Stabiliser (carboxymethylcellulose)
Preservative (potassium sorbate)
Colour (beta-carotene)

a) What is the main ingredient in the squash?

....

b) Why have flavourings and colourings been added to the orange squash?

....

....

c) Do you think this product would be suitable for someone with diabetes? Explain your answer.

....

d) Name an additive that has been added to stop the ingredients from separating.

....

Chemistry 1b — Oils, Earth and Atmosphere

Plate Tectonics

Q1 Below is a letter that Alfred Wegener might have written to a newspaper explaining his ideas. Use your knowledge to fill in the gaps.

Dear Herr Schmidt,

I must reply to your highly flawed article of March 23rd 1915 by telling you of my theory of .... Finally I can explain why the .... of identical plants and animals have been found in seemingly unconnected places such as .... and ....

The current idea of sunken .... between these continents is complete hogwash. I propose that South America and South Africa were once part of a much larger land mass that I have named .... This supercontinent has slowly been drifting apart over millions of years. The pieces are being pushed by tidal forces and the .... of the Earth itself.

I will shortly be publishing a full report of my scientific findings.

Yours faithfully,

A Wegener

Q2 True or false?

	True	False
Wegener found that each continent had its own unrelated collection of plant and animal fossils.	☐	☐
Animals were thought to have crossed between continents using land bridges.	☐	☐
The Earth's continents seem to fit together like a big jigsaw.	☐	☐
Rocks are made of layers, which are different on every continent.	☐	☐
Fossils of tropical plants have been found in places where they shouldn't have survived, like the Arctic.	☐	☐
Pangaea is thought to have existed 3 million years ago.	☐	☐
Most scientists immediately agreed with Wegener's ideas.	☐	☐
Wegener had a PhD in geology.	☐	☐
Investigations of the ocean floor showed that although Wegener wasn't absolutely right, his ideas were pretty close.	☐	☐
Wegener died before his ideas were accepted.	☐	☐

Chemistry 1b — Oils, Earth and Atmosphere

Plate Tectonics

Q3 Wegener's theory of continental drift was put forward after he found **evidence**.
List four pieces of evidence that Wegener found.

1. ....
....

2. ....
....

3. ....
....

4. ....
....
....

Q4 According to Wegener's theory, the continents were moving apart.

a) i) What two forces did Wegener suggest were responsible for the movement of the continents?
....

ii) Why did many scientists say that this was impossible?
....

iii) Give two other reasons why most scientists weren't convinced by Wegener's theory.
....
....

b) Where did scientists finally find evidence that supported Wegener's ideas?
....
....

Chemistry 1b — Oils, Earth and Atmosphere

The Earth's Structure

Q1 Look at the diagram showing the boundary between the African and Arabian plates.

The Red Sea is widening at a speed of 1.6 cm per year.

Remember to include a unit in your answer.

a) If the sea level remains the same, how much will the Red Sea widen in 10 000 years?

....

b) The Red Sea is currently exactly 325 km wide at a certain point. If the sea level remains the same, how wide will the Red Sea be at this point in 20 000 years' time?

....

Don't forget to make sure your distances are in the same unit.

....

Q2 The map below on the left shows where most of the world's earthquakes take place.

● = main earthquake zones

Compare this map to one showing the tectonic plates.
What do you notice about the main earthquake zones?

....

....

Chemistry 1b — Oils, Earth and Atmosphere

The Earth's Structure

Q3 Draw a simple diagram of the Earth's structure.
Label the crust, mantle and core and write a brief description of each.

Q4 Match up the description to the key phrase or word.

Key word	Description
Crust	Hot spots that often sit on plate boundaries
Mantle	A well-known plate boundary in North America
Convection current	Caused by sudden movements of plates
Tectonic plates	Thinnest of the Earth's layers
Eurasian Plate	Caused by radioactive decay in the mantle
Earthquakes	Large pieces of crust and upper mantle
Volcanoes	Slowly flowing semi-solid layer that plates float on
San Andreas Fault	Moving away from the North American Plate but toward the African Plate

Q5 How do scientists predict volcanic eruptions and earthquakes?
Complete the table to show what **evidence** can be collected, and comment on its **reliability**.

	Evidence	How reliable is it?
Earthquake		
Volcanic eruption		

Top Tips: That's the problem with "evidence" predicting earthquakes and volcanic eruptions — it's nowhere near 100% reliable. There are likely to be shed-loads of people living near a volcano or on a fault line — it'd be impossible to evacuate them all every time scientists thought there might possibly be an eruption or an earthquake some time soon — it just wouldn't work.

Chemistry 1b — Oils, Earth and Atmosphere

The Evolution of the Atmosphere

Q1 Tick the boxes next to the sentences below that are **true**.

When the Earth was formed, its surface was molten. ☐

The Earth's early atmosphere is thought to have been mostly oxygen. ☐

When oxygen started building up in the atmosphere, all organisms began to thrive. ☐

When some plants died and were buried under layers of sediment, the carbon they had removed from the atmosphere became locked up as fossil fuels. ☐

The development of the ozone layer meant the Earth's temperature reached a suitable level for complex organisms like us to evolve. ☐

Q2 The amount of **carbon dioxide** in the atmosphere has changed over the last 4.5 billion or so years.

Describe how the level of carbon dioxide has changed and explain why this change happened.

....

....

....

....

Q3 Draw lines to put the statements in the **right order** on the timeline. One is done for you.

Timeline: Present → 4600 million years ago (NOT TO SCALE)

Statements:
- The Earth cooled down slightly. A thin crust formed.
- Water vapour condensed to form oceans.
- The Earth formed. There was lots of volcanic activity.
- More complex organisms evolved.
- Plant life appeared.
- The atmosphere is about four-fifths nitrogen and one-fifth oxygen.
- Oxygen built up due to photosynthesis, and the ozone layer developed.

Don't get confused — 4600 million is the same as 4.6 billion.

Chemistry 1b — Oils, Earth and Atmosphere

The Evolution of the Atmosphere

Q4   The pie chart below shows the proportions of different gases in the Earth's atmosphere today.

a) Add the labels '**Nitrogen**', '**Oxygen**', and '**Carbon dioxide and other gases**'.

b) Give the approximate percentages of the following gases in the air today:

Nitrogen ....

Oxygen ....

c) This pie chart shows the proportions of different gases that we think were in the Earth's atmosphere 4500 million years ago.

Describe the main differences between today's atmosphere and the atmosphere 4500 million years ago.

....

....

d) Explain why the amount of water vapour has decreased.

....

What did the water vapour change into?

....

e) Explain how oxygen was introduced into the atmosphere.

....

f) What were two effects of the rising oxygen levels in the atmosphere?

1. ....

....

2. ....

....

Chemistry 1b — Oils, Earth and Atmosphere

The Evolution of the Atmosphere

Q5 Noble gases are found in our atmosphere.

a) Name the six noble gases.

....

b) In which group of the periodic table are they found? ....

c) What is special about these gases?

....

d) What percentage of our atmosphere do the noble gases make up?

....

e) Write down a use for each of the following noble gases.

Argon: ....

Neon: ....

Helium: ....

Q6 There is a scientific theory that says that the water on Earth came from comets, not volcanoes.

Why is this theory not accepted by many scientists?

....

Think of different types of water.

....

Q7 Scientists now have evidence that the ozone layer is thinning and in places holes have developed. This has been linked to an increase in skin cancer over the past 30 years.

a) Explain why the thinning of the ozone layer is thought to have contributed to the rise in skin cancer.

....

....

b) Do these facts prove that the thinning of the ozone layer has caused the rise in skin cancer cases? Explain your answer.

....

....

Top Tips: Don't jump to conclusions — always look at evidence suspiciously. Think about what else might have caused the effect. Take skin cancer for example — it's increased over the last 30 years, during which time the ozone layer has been thinning. But this doesn't mean that there's definitely a link. There have been lots of lifestyle changes too, and some of these may be responsible.

Chemistry 1b — Oils, Earth and Atmosphere

The Evolution of the Atmosphere

Q8 Answer these questions about the damage to the ozone layer.

a) Over which areas of the Earth have holes in the ozone layer occurred?
....

b) Which gases were the main cause of the holes?
....

c) Name two household products which contained these gases.
....

Q9 The graphs below show the changes in atmospheric carbon dioxide levels and temperature since 1850.

a) i) Name two human activities that are thought to have contributed to the rise in carbon dioxide levels over the last 150 years.

1. ....

2. ....

ii) Do all scientists agree that the increase in carbon dioxide concentration has definitely been caused by these human activities? If not, explain the scientists' reasons.

....

....

b) i) Look at the temperature graph.
Has the temperature increased or decreased as carbon dioxide has risen?

....

ii) Many scientists believe that the temperature has changed because there is more carbon dioxide to trap the Sun's energy. What name is given to gases which trap heat from the Sun?

....

Chemistry 1b — Oils, Earth and Atmosphere

Mixed Questions — Chemistry 1b

Q1 The general formula for an alkene is C_nH_{2n}.

a) **Explain** what this general formula means. ....

....

b) The structural formula for ethene is shown to the right.
Draw the structural formula for pentene in the other box.

c) How do alkenes differ from alkanes?

....

....

Q2 Octane is heated and passed over a catalyst.
It **thermally decomposes** as shown to the right.

octane → hexane + ethene

a) What is the process of splitting up long-chain hydrocarbons by thermal decomposition called?

....

b) **Decane** ($C_{10}H_{22}$) is cracked to produce **propene**.
Write a word equation and a symbol equation to show this.

word equation: ....

symbol equation: ....

c) Describe how ethene can be used to make **ethanol**.

....

d) Suggest **one** other way to make ethanol. What is the advantage of making it this way?

....

....

Q3 Ethene molecules can join together in a **polymerisation** reaction.

a) **Explain** the term '**polymerisation**'.

....

b) Styrene molecules can also join together to form a polymer.
Name this polymer and **draw** a diagram of part of it below.

....

c) **Plastics** are polymers. Most plastics aren't biodegradable. Explain one problem this creates.

....

Chemistry 1b — Oils, Earth and Atmosphere

Mixed Questions — Chemistry 1b

Q4 The **ingredients** list from a tin of **macaroni cheese** is shown below.

> **Macaroni Cheese — Ingredients**
> Water, Durum Wheat, Cheddar Cheese, Rapeseed Oil, Salt, Sugar, Skimmed Milk Powder, Mustard, Stabilisers (Polyphosphates, Sodium Phosphate), Flavour Enhancer (E621), Colour (E160)

Another situation where stabilisers would have held everything together.

a) **i)** Explain why E160 has been added to the macaroni cheese.

....

ii) A food magazine reported that two readers suffered headaches after eating the macaroni cheese. They concluded that additives such as E160 are harmful to health. Discuss whether this conclusion is valid.

....

....

b) **i)** Which ingredient in the macaroni cheese is likely to contain the most saturated fat?
....

Animal products tend to contain more saturated fat.

ii) Name a **health problem** that too much saturated fat can cause?

....

c) **i)** The macaroni cheese contains rapeseed oil, which is a vegetable oil. It is mostly a monounsaturated oil. What does the term "**monounsaturated**" mean?

....

ii) Circle the correct word or words to complete this sentence.

Rapeseed oil <u>will</u> / <u>will not</u> decolourise bromine water.

iii) Vegetable oils can be mixed with water to form **emulsions**. Give two examples of foods that contain emulsions.

....

Q5 People used to think that the Earth's surface was all one piece. Today, we think it's made up of **separate plates** of rock.

a) It wasn't until the 1960s that geologists were convinced that this was the case. Suggest why there was little evidence to support the theory before the 1960s.

....

....

b) What is thought to cause the **movement** of the plates?

....

c) Name **two** kinds of natural disasters that can occur at the boundaries between plates.

.... and ....

Chemistry 1b — Oils, Earth and Atmosphere

Mixed Questions — Chemistry 1b

Q6 The graphs below give information about the Earth's atmosphere millions of years ago and today.

No one is certain about the exact composition of the early atmosphere so these figures are rough estimates.

a) Could the early atmosphere **support life** as we know it? Explain your answer.

....

....

b) Which **organisms** caused an increase in oxygen and a decrease in carbon dioxide?

....

c) Even though the level of **carbon dioxide** is much lower now than millions of years ago, in the last 250 years the level has **increased**. Complete the following passage by circling the correct words.

> Humans are **increasing** / **decreasing** the amount of **carbon dioxide** / **oxygen** in the atmosphere by **burning** / **creating** fossil fuels. Also, deforestation **reduces** / **increases** the amount of carbon dioxide **absorbed** / **released** from the atmosphere.

d) **i)** **Biodiesel** is a renewable fuel. What is it made from? ....

    ii) Explain why burning biodiesel produces **no net increase** in atmospheric carbon dioxide.

....

....

    iii) Give one reason why biodiesel isn't widely used at the moment.

....

e) Tick the correct boxes to indicate whether each statement is **true** or **false**.

                                                                                                           True False

    i) 5% of the atmosphere is noble gases.

    ii) The amount of ozone in the ozone layer is decreasing.

    iii) Very early in Earth's history volcanoes gave out gases.

    iv) Scientists are good at predicting volcanoes and earthquakes.

Chemistry 1b — Oils, Earth and Atmosphere

Chemistry 2(i) — Bonding and Reactions

Atoms

Q1 **Complete** the following sentences.

a) Neutral atoms have a .... charge.

b) A charged atom is called an ....

c) A neutral atom has the same number of .... and ....

d) If an electron is added to a neutral atom, the atom becomes .... charged.

Q2 **Complete** this table.

Particle	Mass	Charge
Proton	1	
	1	0
Electron		−1

Q3 **What am I?**

Choose from: **nucleus   proton   electron   neutron**

a) I am in the centre of the atom. I contain protons and neutrons. ....

b) I move around the nucleus in a shell. ....

c) I am the lightest. ....

d) I am positively charged. ....

e) I am heavy and have no charge. ....

f) In a neutral atom there are as many of me as there are electrons. ....

Q4 Elements have a **mass number** and an **atomic number**.

a) What does the **mass number** of an element tell you about its atoms?

....

b) What does the **atomic number** of an element tell you about its atoms?

....

c) Fill in this table using a periodic table.

Element	Symbol	Mass Number	Number of Protons	Number of Electrons	Number of Neutrons
Sodium	Na		11		
		16	8	8	8
Neon			10	10	10
	Ca			20	20

Chemistry 2(i) — Bonding and Reactions

Elements, Compounds and Isotopes

Q1 a) Correctly label the following diagrams as either '**element**' or '**compound**'.

A = ... B = ... C = ... D = ...

b) Suggest which diagram (A, B, C or D) could represent:

i) oxygen .... ii) sodium .... iii) sodium chloride .... iv) carbon dioxide ....

Q2 Circle the **correct words** in these sentences.

a) **Compounds / Atoms** are formed when two or more elements react together.

b) The properties of compounds are **exactly the same as / completely different to** the original elements.

c) It is **easy / difficult** to separate the elements in a compound.

d) Carbon dioxide is **a compound / an element**, whereas iron is **a compound / an element**.

e) The number of **neutrons / electrons** determines the chemistry of an element.

Q3 Choose the correct words to **complete** this paragraph.

| electrons | element | isotopes | protons | compound | neutrons |

.... are different atomic forms of the same .... which have the same number of .... but a different number of ....

Q4 Which of the following atoms are **isotopes** of each other? Explain your answer.

W $^{12}_{6}C$ X $^{4}_{2}He$ Y $^{14}_{6}C$ Z $^{14}_{7}N$

Answer .... and ....

Explanation ....

Q5 Explain why **carbon-14** (an unstable isotope) is very useful to **historians**.

....

....

Chemistry 2(i) — Bonding and Reactions

The Periodic Table

Q1 Select from these **elements** to answer the following questions.

iodine, nickel, silicon, sodium, radon, krypton, calcium

a) Which two are in the same group? .... and ....

b) Name an alkali metal. ....

c) Name a transition metal. ....

d) Name an element with seven electrons in its outer shell. ....

e) Name a non-metal which is not in group 0. ....

Q2 **True** or **false**?

	True	False
a) Elements in the same **group** have the same number of electrons in their outer shell.	☐	☐
b) The periodic table shows the elements in order of ascending **atomic mass**.	☐	☐
c) Each **column** in the periodic table contains elements with similar properties.	☐	☐
d) The periodic table is made up of all the known compounds.	☐	☐
e) There are more than 100 known elements.	☐	☐

Q3 Elements in the same group undergo **similar reactions**.

a) Tick the pairs of elements that would undergo similar reactions.

A potassium and rubidium ☐   C calcium and oxygen ☐

B helium and fluorine ☐   D calcium and magnesium ☐

b) Explain why fluorine and chlorine undergo similar reactions.

....

....

Q4 Complete the following table.

	Alternative Name for Group	Number of Electrons in Outer Shell
Group I	Alkali metals	
Group VII		7
Group 0		*

* excluding helium

Chemistry 2(i) — Bonding and Reactions

Electron Shells

Q1 a) Tick the boxes to show whether each statement is **true** or **false**.

        i) Electrons occupy shells in atoms.

        ii) The highest energy levels are always filled first.

        iii) Atoms are most stable when they have partially filled shells.

        iv) Noble gases have a full outer shell of electrons.

        v) Reactive elements have full outer shells.

b) Write out corrected versions of the **false** statements.

....

....

....

Q2 Describe **two** things that are wrong with this diagram.

1. ....

....

2. ....

....

Q3 Write out the **electron configurations** for the following elements.

    a) Beryllium ....   **d)** Calcium ....

    b) Oxygen ....   **e)** Aluminium ....

    c) Silicon ....   **f)** Argon ....

Q4 Do the following groups of elements contain **reactive** or **unreactive** elements? Explain your answers in terms of **electron shells**.

    a) Noble gases ....

....

    b) Alkali metals ....

....

Chemistry 2(i) — Bonding and Reactions

Electron Shells

Q5 **Chlorine has an atomic number of 17.**

a) What is its electron configuration? ....

b) Draw the electrons on the shells in the diagram.

c) Why does chlorine react readily?

....

Q6 Draw the **full electron configurations** for these elements. (The first three have been done for you.)

Hydrogen

Helium

Lithium

a) Carbon

b) Nitrogen

c) Fluorine

d) Sodium

e) Magnesium

f) Phosphorus

g) Sulfur

h) Potassium

i) Calcium

Top Tips: Once you've learnt the 'electron shell rules' these are pretty easy — the first shell can only take 2 electrons, and the second and third shells a maximum of 8 each. Don't forget it.

Chemistry 2(i) — Bonding and Reactions

Ionic Bonding

Q1 True or false?

		True	False
a)	In ionic bonding, atoms lose or gain electrons.	☐	☐
b)	Ions with opposite charges attract each other.	☐	☐
c)	Ionic bonds always produce giant ionic structures.	☐	☐
d)	Ions in a giant ionic structure are loosely packed together.	☐	☐
e)	Ionic compounds dissolve to form solutions that conduct electricity.	☐	☐

Q2 Use the **diagram** to answer the following questions.

a) Which **group** of the periodic table does **sodium** belong to? ....

b) How many **electrons** does **chlorine** need to gain to get a full outer shell of electrons? ....

c) What is the **charge** on a **sodium ion**? ....

d) What is the chemical formula of **sodium chloride**? ....

Q3 Elements react in order to get a **full outer shell** of electrons.

a) How many electrons does magnesium need to **lose** to get a full outer shell? ....

b) How many electrons does oxygen need to **gain** to get a full outer shell? ....

c) Draw a 'dot and cross' diagram to show what happens to the outer shells of electrons when magnesium and oxygen react.

The diagrams in question 2 are 'dot and cross' diagrams.

d) What is the chemical formula of magnesium oxide? ....

e) What type of **structure** would you expect magnesium oxide to have? ....

Chemistry 2(i) — Bonding and Reactions

Ionic Bonding

Q4 Sodium chloride (salt) has a **giant ionic structure**.

a) Circle the correct words to explain why sodium chloride has a high melting point.

> Salt has very **strong** / **weak** chemical bonds between the **negative** / **positive** sodium ions and the **negative** / **positive** chlorine ions. This means that it needs a **little** / **large** amount of energy to break the bonds.

b) Name two other **properties** of compounds with **giant ionic structures**.

1. ....

2. ....

Q5 Here are some elements and the ions they form:

beryllium, Be^{2+}   **potassium, K^+**   **iodine, I^-**   **sulfur, S^{2-}**

Make sure the charges on the ions balance.

Write down the formulas of four compounds which can be made using these elements.

1. ....   2. ....

3. ....   4. ....

Q6 Mike conducts an experiment to find out if **calcium chloride** conducts electricity. He tests the compound when it's solid, when it's dissolved in water and when it's molten.

a) Complete the following table of results.

	Conducts electricity?
When solid	
When dissolved in water	
When molten	

b) Explain your answers to part a).

....

....

....

Top Tips: Giant ionic structures are the first of four different types of structure that you need to know about. You'll have to be able to identify the structure in different compounds later on — so make sure you can describe and recognise their properties now.

Chemistry 2(i) — Bonding and Reactions

Electron Shells and Ions

Q1 Complete the following sentences by circling the correct words.

a) Atoms that have lost or gained electrons are called **isotopes** / **ions**.

b) Elements in Group 1 **readily** / **rarely** form ions.

c) Elements in Group 8 **readily** / **rarely** form ions.

d) Positive ions are called **anions** / **cations**.

Q2 Atoms can **gain** or **lose** electrons to get a full outer shell.

a) How many **electrons** do the following elements need to **lose** in order to get a **full outer shell**.

i) Lithium .... ii) Calcium .... iii) Potassium ....

b) How many **electrons** do the following elements need to **gain** in order to get a **full outer shell**.

i) Oxygen .... ii) Chlorine .... iii) Fluorine ....

Q3 Write the **electron configurations** for the following ions and draw the **electrons** on the shells. (The first one's been done for you.)

Na⁺ Na [2,8]⁺

a) Cl⁻ ....

b) Mg²⁺ ....

c) O²⁻ ....

Q4 What are the **electron configurations** of the following ions?

a) K⁺ ....   b) Ca²⁺ ....

c) F⁻ ....   d) Be²⁺ ....

Chemistry 2(i) — Bonding and Reactions

Covalent Bonding

Q1 Indicate whether each statement is **true** or **false**.

                                                                                           True False

- a) Covalent bonding involves sharing electrons.
- b) Atoms react to gain a full outer shell of electrons.
- c) Some atoms can make both ionic and covalent bonds.
- d) Hydrogen can form two covalent bonds.
- e) Carbon can form four covalent bonds.

Q2 **Complete** the following table to show how many electrons are needed to **fill up** the **outer shell** of these atoms.

Atom	Carbon	Chlorine	Hydrogen	Nitrogen	Oxygen
Number of electrons needed to fill outer shell					

Q3 Complete the following diagrams by adding the **electrons**. Only the outer shells are shown.

- a) Hydrogen chloride (HCl)
- b) Oxygen (O_2)
- c) Water (H_2O)
- d) Ammonia (NH_3)
- e) Methane (CH_4)

Q4 Why do some atoms **share** electrons?

....

....

Chemistry 2(i) — Bonding and Reactions

Covalent Substances: Two Kinds

Q1 Which am I — **diamond**, **graphite** or **silicon dioxide** (silica)?

Match up the statements to the drawings.

- I am used in jewellery.
- I am used to make glass.
- I am the hardest natural substance.
- I have layers which move over one another.
- I am used in pencils.
- I am the only non-metal which is a good conductor of electricity.
- I am known as sand.
- I am not made from carbon.
- My carbon atoms form three covalent bonds.
- My carbon atoms form four covalent bonds.

Diamond

Graphite

Silicon dioxide

Q2 Circle the correct words to complete the following paragraph.

Giant covalent structures contain **charged ions / uncharged atoms**. The covalent bonds between the atoms are **strong / weak**. Giant covalent structures have **high / low** melting points, they usually **do / don't** conduct electricity and they are usually **soluble / insoluble** in water.

Q3 Hydrogen and chlorine share electrons to form a molecule called **hydrogen chloride**.

Predict two properties hydrogen chloride will have.

1. ....

2. ....

Q4 **Graphite** and **diamond** are both entirely made from **carbon**, but have different properties.

a) Explain why graphite is a good conductor of electricity.

....

....

b) Explain why diamond's structure makes it hard.

....

....

Chemistry 2(i) — Bonding and Reactions

Metallic Structures

Q1 **Complete** the following sentences about metals.

a) Metals have a giant .... structure.

b) Metals are good conductors of .... and ....

c) The atoms in metals can slide over each other, so metals are ....

Q2 How do metals **conduct electricity**?

....

....

Q3 Use the information below to choose a suitable metal for each of the following uses. **Explain** your choice.

Metal	Melting Point (°C)	Specific Heat Capacity (J/Kg/°C)	Density	Electrical Conductivity	Reaction with Water
A	659	900	low	good	none
B	1539	470	average	average	slight
C	98	1222	very low	average	very vigorous
D	183	130	average	excellent	none
E	3377	135	very high	average	none

a) A filament for a **household light bulb**. ....

The temperature of household light bulb filaments can reach 2500 °C.

....

b) A metal used for making **aeroplanes**. ....

....

c) A coolant for a **nuclear reactor**. ....

....

d) An overhead **power cable**. ....

....

Power cables need to have a low density.

Chemistry 2(i) — Bonding and Reactions

Metallic Structures

Q4 What type of **structure** is present in substances which:

Choose from giant ionic, giant covalent, simple molecular or metallic.

a) Don't conduct electricity when solid, but do when liquid. ....

b) Have high melting points and don't conduct electricity when molten. ....

c) Conduct electricity when solid and liquid. ....

Q5 Complete the following table by placing a **tick** or a **cross** in each box.

Property	Giant Ionic	Giant Covalent	Simple Molecular	Metallic
High melting and boiling points				
Can conduct electricity when solid		except graphite		
Can conduct electricity when molten		except graphite		

Q6 The **properties** of four substances are given below.

Substance	Melting Point (°C)	Good Electrical Conductor?
A	2000	Only when molten and dissolved
B	2500	No
C	20	No
D	600	Yes

Identify the **structure** of each substance. Explain your choice.

a) Substance A ....

....

b) Substance B ....

....

c) Substance C ....

....

d) Substance D ....

....

Chemistry 2(i) — Bonding and Reactions

New Materials

Q1 **Buckminster fullerene** is made up of 60 carbon atoms.

a) What is the **molecular formula** of buckminster fullerene? ....

b) How many covalent bonds does each carbon atom form? ....

c) Can buckminster fullerene conduct electricity? Explain your answer.

....

....

Q2 **Smart materials** have some really weird properties.

a) What are **smart materials**?

....

b) Choose from the words below to complete the paragraph.

| gases | liquids | solid | dyes | contract | temperature | evaporate |

Smart materials include .... that change colour depending on the ...., ... that turn .... when you place them in a magnetic field, and other materials that expand or .... when you put an electric current through them.

Q3 Nanoparticles are really tiny particles, between 1 and 100 nanometres across.

a) How many nanometres are there in **1 mm**?

1 nm = 0.000 001 mm

....

....

b) Explain how nanoparticles are useful in producing industrial **catalysts**.

....

....

c) Nanoparticles are used to build surfaces with very specific properties. Describe a use of this technology and give an example.

....

....

Chemistry 2(i) — Bonding and Reactions

New Materials

Q4 **Nitinol is a shape memory alloy.**

a) True or false?

    i) Nitinol is made from nickel and silver.   □ □

    ii) Nitinol is a mixture of metals.   □ □

    iii) When cool, nitinol can bend and twist like rubber.   □ □

b) Write out corrected versions of any **false** statements.

....

....

c) Explain why nitinol is called a 'shape memory alloy'.

....

....

d) What is nitinol used for?

....

Q5 **Fullerenes can be joined together to make nanotubes.**

a) What are nanotubes?

....

b) Give two properties of nanotubes that make them useful as **electrical circuits** in computers.

....

....

c) Give a property of nanotubes that makes them useful in **tennis rackets**?

....

Q6 **What is molecular engineering?**

....

....

....

Top Tips: Scientists have made nanostructures from DNA that look like smiley faces — each one a thousandth of the width of a human hair. They've also made a nanomap of the Americas.

Chemistry 2(i) — Bonding and Reactions

Relative Formula Mass

Q1 a) What is meant by the **relative atomic mass** of an element?

....

b) What are the **relative atomic masses** (A_r) of the following:

i) magnesium .... iv) hydrogen .... vii) K ....

ii) neon .... v) C .... viii) Ca ....

iii) oxygen .... vi) Cu .... ix) Cl ....

Q2 Identify the elements A, B and C.

> Element A has an A_r of 4.
> Element B has an A_r 3 times that of element A.
> Element C has an A_r 4 times that of element A.

Element A is ....

Element B is ....

Element C is ....

Q3 a) Explain how the **relative formula mass** of a **compound** is calculated.

....

b) What are the **relative formula masses** (M_r) of the following:

i) water (H_2O) ....

ii) potassium hydroxide (KOH) ....

iii) nitric acid (HNO_3) ....

iv) sulfuric acid (H_2SO_4) ....

v) ammonium nitrate (NH_4NO_3) ....

Q4 The equation below shows a reaction between element X and water. The total M_r of the products is **114**. What is substance X?

$$2X + 2H_2O \rightarrow 2XOH + H_2$$

....

....

Top Tips: The periodic table really comes in useful here. There's no way you'll be able to answer these questions without one (unless you've memorised all the elements' relative atomic masses — and that would just be silly). And lucky for you, you'll get given one in your exam. Yay!

Chemistry 2(i) — Bonding and Reactions

Two Formula Mass Calculations

Q1 a) Write down the **formula** for calculating the **percentage mass** of an element in a compound.

......

b) Calculate the percentage mass of the following elements in ammonium nitrate, NH_4NO_3.

i) Nitrogen ......

ii) Hydrogen ......

iii) Oxygen ......

Q2 **Nitrogen monoxide**, NO, reacts with oxygen, O_2, to form **oxide R**.

a) Calculate the percentage mass of nitrogen in **nitrogen monoxide**.

......

b) Oxide R has a percentage composition by mass of **30.4% nitrogen** and **69.6% oxygen**. Work out its empirical formula.

......

Q3 1.48 g of a **calcium compound** contains 0.8 g of calcium, 0.64 g of oxygen and 0.04 g of hydrogen. Work out the empirical formula of the compound.

......

Q4 a) Calculate the percentage mass of **oxygen** in each of the following compounds.

    A Fe_2O_3 **B** H_2O **C** $CaCO_3$

b) Which compound has the **greatest** percentage mass of oxygen? ......

Chemistry 2(i) — Bonding and Reactions

Calculating Masses in Reactions

Q1 Anna burns **10 g** of **magnesium** in air to produce **magnesium oxide** (MgO).

a) Write out the **balanced equation** for this reaction.

....

b) Calculate the mass of **magnesium oxide** that's produced.

....

....

....

Q2 What mass of **sodium** is needed to make **2 g** of **sodium oxide**? $4Na + O_2 \rightarrow 2Na_2O$

....

....

....

Q3 **Aluminium** and **iron oxide** (Fe_2O_3) react together to produce **aluminium oxide** (Al_2O_3) and **iron**.

a) Write out the **balanced equation** for this reaction.

....

b) What **mass** of iron is produced from **20 g** of iron oxide?

....

....

....

Q4 When heated, **limestone** ($CaCO_3$) decomposes to form **calcium oxide** (CaO) and **carbon dioxide**.

How many **kilograms** of limestone are needed to make **100 kilograms** of **calcium oxide**?

The calculation is exactly the same — just use 'kg' instead of 'g'.

....

....

....

....

Chemistry 2(i) — Bonding and Reactions

Calculating Masses in Reactions

Q5 Iron oxide is reduced to iron inside a blast furnace using carbon. There are three stages involved.

Stage A $\quad C + O_2 \rightarrow CO_2$

Stage B $\quad CO_2 + C \rightarrow 2CO$

Stage C $\quad 3CO + Fe_2O_3 \rightarrow 2Fe + 3CO_2$

a) If **10 g** of **carbon** are used in stage B, and all the carbon monoxide produced gets used in stage C, what **mass** of CO_2 is produced in **stage C**?

....

Work out the mass of CO at the end of stage B first.

....

....

....

b) Suggest how the CO_2 might be used after stage C?

....

Look at where CO_2 is used.

Q6 **Sodium sulfate** (Na_2SO_4) is made by reacting **sodium hydroxide** (NaOH) with **sulfuric acid** (H_2SO_4). **Water** is also produced.

a) Write out the **balanced equation** for this reaction.

....

b) What mass of **sodium hydroxide** is needed to make **75 g** of **sodium sulfate**?

....

....

....

....

c) What mass of **water** is formed when **50 g** of **sulfuric acid** reacts?

....

....

....

Chemistry 2(i) — Bonding and Reactions

The Mole

Q1 a) **Complete** the following sentence.

> One mole of atoms or molecules of any substance will have a .... in grams equal to the .... for that substance.

b) What is the mass of each of the following?

i) 1 mole of copper. ....

ii) 3 moles of chlorine **gas**. ....

iii) 2 mole of nitric acid (HNO_3). ....

iv) 0.5 moles of calcium carbonate ($CaCO_3$). ....

Q2 a) What is the **volume** of **one mole** of any gas at room temperature and pressure? Circle your answer.

        24 litres   12 litres   2.4 litres   36 litres

b) What volume is occupied by the following gases at room temperature and pressure?

i) 4.5 moles of oxygen. ....

ii) 2.4 moles of chlorine. ....

iii) 0.48 moles of hydrogen. ....

Q3 a) Write down the formula for calculating the **number of moles in a solution**.

b) Use the formula to calculate the number of moles in: *There are 1000 cm^3 in 1 litre.*

i) 50 cm^3 of a 2M solution. ....

ii) 250 cm^3 of a 0.5M solution. ....

iii) 550 cm^3 of a 1.75M solution. ....

c) **200 cm^3** of a solution contains **0.25 moles** of iron hydroxide. Calculate its **molar concentration**.

....

d) What **volume** of a 1.5M solution of calcium hydroxide contains **2 moles** of calcium hydroxide?

....

Chemistry 2(i) — Bonding and Reactions

The Mole

Q4 a) Write down the formula for calculating the **number of moles in a given mass**.

  b) How many **moles** are there in each of the following?

   i) 20 g of calcium. ....

   ii) 112 g of sulfur. ....

   iii) 200 g of copper oxide (CuO). ....

  c) Calculate the **mass** of each of the following.

   i) 2 moles of sodium. ....

   ii) 0.75 moles of magnesium oxide (MgO). ....

   iii) 0.025 moles of lead chloride (PbCl$_2$). ....

Q5 Ali adds **13 g** of zinc to **50 cm³** of hydrochloric acid. All the zinc reacts.

$$Zn + 2HCl \rightarrow ZnCl_2 + H_2$$

  a) How many moles of zinc were added?

   ....

  b) How many moles of hydrochloric acid reacted?

   Look at the symbol equation.

   ....

Q6 Danni adds **0.6 g** of magnesium to sulfuric acid. Magnesium sulfate and hydrogen form. All the magnesium reacts.

  a) Write a **balanced symbol equation** for this reaction.

   ....

  b) What **volume** of hydrogen was produced?

   ....

   ....

  c) Calculate the **mass** of magnesium sulfate produced.

   ....

   ....

Chemistry 2(i) — Bonding and Reactions

Atom Economy

Q1 **Copper oxide** can be reduced to copper by burning it with carbon.

copper ore + carbon → copper + carbon dioxide

$2CuO + C \rightarrow 2Cu + CO_2$

a) What is the useful product in this reaction? ....

b) Calculate the atom economy.

$$\text{atom economy} = \frac{\text{total } M_r \text{ of useful products}}{\text{total } M_r \text{ of reactants}} \times 100$$

....

c) What percentage of the starting materials are wasted?

....

Q2 It is important in industry to find the **best atom economy**.

a) Explain why. ....

....

....

b) What types of reaction have the highest atom economy? Give an example.

....

Q3 **Titanium** can be reduced from titanium chloride ($TiCl_4$) using magnesium or sodium.

a) Work out the atom economy for each reaction.

With magnesium: $TiCl_4 + 2Mg \rightarrow Ti + 2MgCl_2$ ....

....

With sodium: $TiCl_4 + 4Na \rightarrow Ti + 4NaCl$ ....

....

b) Which one has the better atom economy? ....

Q4 **Chromium** can be extracted from its oxide (Cr_2O_3) using **aluminium**. **Aluminium oxide** and **chromium** are formed.

Calculate the atom economy of this reaction.

....

....

Chemistry 2(i) — Bonding and Reactions

Percentage Yield

Q1 James wanted to produce **silver chloride** (AgCl). He added a carefully measured mass of silver nitrate to an excess of dilute hydrochloric acid. An **insoluble white salt** formed.

a) Write down the formula for calculating the **percentage yield** of a reaction.

b) James calculated that he should get 2.7 g of silver chloride, but he only got 1.2 g. What was the **percentage yield**?

....

....

Q2 Explain how the following factors affect the percentage yield.

a) Reversible reactions ....

....

b) Filtration (when you want to keep the liquid) ....

....

c) Transferring liquids ....

....

d) Unexpected reactions ....

....

Q3 Aaliya and Natasha mixed together barium chloride ($BaCl_2$) and sodium sulfate (Na_2SO_4) in a beaker. An **insoluble** substance formed. They **filtered** the solution to obtain the solid substance, and then transferred the solid to a clean piece of **filter paper** and left it to dry.

a) Aaliya calculated that they should produce a yield of **15 g** of barium sulfate. However, after completing the experiment they found they had only obtained **6 g**.

Calculate the **percentage yield** for this reaction.

....

....

b) Suggest **two** reasons why their actual yield was lower than their predicted yield.

1. ....

2. ....

Chemistry 2(i) — Bonding and Reactions

Mixed Questions — Chemistry 2(i)

Q1 Three forms of the element carbon are shown in the diagram.

• carbon atoms

a) Identify the different forms by name.

R .... S .... T ....

b) Form **R** has a melting point of 3652 °C. Form **S** has a melting point of 3550 °C.

i) Explain why forms R and S have very high melting points.
You should mention structure and bonding in your answer.

....

....

ii) Predict whether the melting point of form **T** will be greater than, the same as, or lower than those of the other two forms. Justify your answer.

....

....

Q2 Orwell found that 1.4 g of silicon reacted with 7.1 g of chlorine to produce the reactive liquid silicon chloride.

a) Work out the **empirical formula** of the silicon chloride.

....

....

b) Calculate the **percentage mass** of chlorine in silicon chloride.

....

....

c) Write down the balanced chemical equation for the reaction.

....

d) Orwell predicted he would obtain 8.5 g of silicon chloride, however he only obtained 6.5 g. Calculate the percentage yield for this reaction.

....

e) Does this reaction have a high atom economy? Explain your answer.

....

Chemistry 2(i) — Bonding and Reactions

Mixed Questions — Chemistry 2(i)

Q3 **Calcium** is a reactive metal in **Group II** of the periodic table.

a) Give the electron arrangements in a calcium **atom** and a calcium **ion**, Ca^{2+}.

Electron arrangement in a Ca atom ....

Electron arrangement in a Ca^{2+} ion ....

b) The **mass number** of the main isotope of calcium is 40.
Use the periodic table to determine the number of **neutrons** in the nucleus of this isotope.

....

c) Name an element which has similar properties to calcium. ....

Q4 The table gives data for some physical properties of a selection of elements and compounds.

substance	state at room temp	melting point / °C	boiling point / °C	electrical conductivity solid	electrical conductivity liquid
A	solid	114	184	poor	poor
B	gas	-73	-10	poor	poor
C	solid	3550	4827	poor	poor
D	solid	858	1505	poor	good
E	solid	1495	2870	good	good
F	liquid	0	50	poor	poor

a) Identify one substance that is **likely** to have a **simple molecular** structure. Justify your answer.

....

b) Which of the substances is **most likely** to have a **giant covalent** structure? ....

c) Explain why substance D is **unlikely** to be a **metallic** element.

....

Q5 Magnesium reacts with nitric acid (HNO_3) to form magnesium nitrate ($Mg(NO_3)_2$).

a) Work out the **relative formula mass** of magnesium nitrate.

....

b) When 0.12 g of magnesium reacted with excess acid, 0.74 g of magnesium nitrate was formed.

i) Calculate the **number of moles** of magnesium and magnesium nitrate.

....

ii) The total volume of the solution formed was 0.2 dm^3. Work out the **concentration** of magnesium nitrate in this solution using your answer from part i).

....

c) If 0.025 moles of nitric acid was used, what **mass** of nitric acid was this?

....

Chemistry 2(i) — Bonding and Reactions

Rates of Reaction

Q1 The five statements below are about **rates of reaction**.
Circle the correct words to complete the sentences.

a) The **higher** / **lower** the temperature the faster the rate of reaction.

b) A **higher** / **lower** concentration will reduce the rate of reaction.

c) If the reactants are **gases** / **liquids**, the higher the pressure the **faster** / **slower** the rate of reaction.

d) A smaller particle size **increases** / **decreases** the rate of reaction.

e) A catalyst changes the rate of reaction but **is** / **isn't** used up.

Q2 In an experiment, **different sizes** of marble chips were reacted with excess hydrochloric acid. The **same mass** of marble was used each time. The graph below shows how much **gas** was produced when using large marble chips (X), medium marble chips (Y) and small marble chips (Z).

a) i) Which curve (X, Y or Z) shows the **fastest** reaction? Circle the correct answer.

    X   Y   Z

ii) How can you tell this by looking at the graph?

....

....

b) Why is an **excess** of acid used? ....

c) Why do all the reactions produce the **same** volume of gas?

....

d) On the graph, draw the curve you would expect to see if you used **more** of the small marble chips. Assume that all the other conditions are the same as before.

Q3 Another experiment investigated the **change in mass** of the reactants during a reaction in which a **gas** was given off. The graph below shows the results for three experiments carried out under different conditions.

a) Does the mass of the reactants **increase** or **decrease**?

   ....

b) Suggest **why** reaction R has a greater change in mass than reactions P and Q.

....

....

c) Suggest what might have caused the difference between reaction P and reaction Q.

....

Measuring Rates of Reaction

Q1 Use the words provided to complete the sentences below about measuring rates of reaction.

faster   speed   volume   reactants   gas   mass   formed   precipitation

a) The .... of a reaction can be measured by observing either how quickly the .... are used up or how quickly the products are ....

b) In a .... reaction you usually measure how quickly the product is formed. The product turns the solution cloudy. The .... it turns cloudy the quicker the reaction.

c) In a reaction that produces a .... you can measure how quickly the .... of the reactants changes or measure the .... of gas given off in a certain time interval.

Q2 Sam conducted an experiment with equal masses of marble chips and equal volumes of hydrochloric acid (HCl). He used two **different concentrations** of acid and measured the **change in mass** of the reactants. Below is a graph of the results.

a) **Circle** the letter(s) to show the **valid conclusion(s)** you might draw from this graph.

A   Rate of reaction depends on the temperature of the reactants.

B   Increasing the concentration of the acid has no effect on the rate of reaction.

C   Rate of reaction depends on the acid concentration.

D   Rate of reactions depends on the mass of the marble chips.

b) **Calculate** the rate of reaction at points K and L on the graph.

i) Rate at point K ....

ii) Rate at point L ....

Don't forget the units.

Chemistry 2(ii) — Rates of Reaction

Measuring Rates of Reaction

Q3 Charlie was comparing the rate of reaction of 5g of magnesium ribbon with 20 ml of **five different concentrations** of hydrochloric acid. Each time he measured how much **gas** was produced during the **first minute** of the reaction. He did the experiment **twice** for each concentration of acid and obtained these results:

Concentration of HCl (mol/dm^3)	Experiment 1 — volume of gas produced (cm^3)	Experiment 2 — volume of gas produced (cm^3)	Average volume of gas produced (cm^3)
2	92	96	
1.5	63	65	
1	44	47	
0.5	20	50	
0.25	9	9	

a) **Fill in** the last column of the table.

The anomalous result is the one that doesn't seem to fit in.

b) Circle the **anomalous** result in the table.

c) Which concentration of hydrochloric acid produced the fastest rate of reaction? ....

d) A diagram of the **apparatus** used in the experiment is shown on the left.

  i) What is the object marked **X** called?

  ....

  ii) Name one other key piece of apparatus needed for this experiment (not shown in the diagram).

  ....

e) **Sketch** a graph of the average volume of gas produced from this investigation against concentration of HCl and **label** the axes. Do not include the anomalous result.

You don't need to plot the values, just draw what the graph would look like.

f) Why did Charlie do the experiment twice and calculate the average volume?

....

g) How might the **anomalous** result have come about?

....

h) Suggest **two changes** Charlie could make to improve his results if he repeated his investigation:

1. ....

2. ....

Chemistry 2(ii) — Rates of Reaction

Rate of Reaction Experiments

Q1 Choose from the words below to complete the paragraph.

surface area   slower   react   decrease   faster   increase

When you crush up a large solid into powder, you .... its surface area. This means it reacts .... Large lumps have a smaller ...., so they .... more slowly.

Q2 Matilda conducted an experiment to investigate the effect of **surface area** on rate of reaction. She added dilute hydrochloric acid to **large marble chips** and measured the volume of gas produced at regular time intervals. She repeated the experiment using the same mass of **powdered marble**. Below is a graph of her results.

a) Which curve, A or B, was obtained when **large pieces** of marble were used? ....

b) On the graph opposite, draw the curve you would get if you used the **same mass** of **medium** sized marble pieces. Label it C.

c) Complete the equation for this reaction.

$CaCO_3 + 2HCl \rightarrow$ .... + ... + H_2O

The chemical name for marble is calcium carbonate.

d) Name the **independent** variable in this investigation. ....

e) Is there enough information given above for you to be sure whether this was a **fair test** or not? Explain your answer.

....

....

f) Which other method(s) could you use to measure the rate of this reaction? Tick the correct one(s).

☐ Timing how long the reaction takes to go cloudy.
☐ Counting how many bubbles are produced per minute.
☐ Timing how long the reaction takes to start.
☐ Measuring how quickly the reaction loses mass.

Chemistry 2(ii) — Rates of Reaction

Rate of Reaction Experiments

Q3 Dillon investigated the reaction between **magnesium** and excess dilute **hydrochloric acid**. He conducted the experiment using **different concentrations** of acid. He recorded the mass of the reactants every 10 seconds for 2 minutes and calculated the change in mass for each reading.

a) How many readings did he take for each concentration? ....

b) Suggest the labels (including units) that he might use for a graph of his results:

x-axis ....

y-axis ....

c) On these axes, draw and label sketches of the curves you would expect for a **high** and a **low** concentration of acid.

d) Here is one of Dillon's results:

> original mass of reactants: 145.73 g
>
> mass of reactants at 1 minute 40 seconds: 143.89 g

Don't forget to include the units.

Calculate the **change** in mass ....

Q4 Here is a graph which has been obtained from a rate of reaction investigation.

a) Which reaction has the highest **initial** rate of reaction? Explain your answer.

....
....
....

b) Circle the **part** of the line for reaction 1 which shows the initial part of the reaction.

c) Why do all the curves level out eventually?

....

Top Tips: Don't forget you can measure the rate of the magnesium and HCl reaction using a gas syringe too, just like the marble chips and HCl reaction — you measure the volume of gas given off.

Chemistry 2(ii) — Rates of Reaction

Rate of Reaction Experiments

Q5 When you mix **sodium thiosulfate** solution and **hydrochloric acid**, a precipitate is formed. Underline the correct statement(s) about the reaction.

All the reactants are soluble.

All the products are soluble.

The precipitate is yellow.   *Sulfur is yellow.*

The mixture goes cloudy.

Q6 Yasmin investigates the effect of **temperature** on the rate of the reaction between sodium thiosulfate and hydrochloric acid. She mixes the reactants together in a flask and times how long a cross placed under the flask takes to disappear.

a) Underline the items from the following list that she could use to do this.

| conical flask   balance   condenser   water bath   stopclock   thermometer |

b) Here are some results from her investigation:

Temperature (°C)	20	30	40	50	60
Time taken for cross to disappear (s)	201	177		112	82

i) As the temperature increases, does the reaction get **faster** or **slower**? ....

ii) One of the values in the table is missing. Circle the most likely value for it from the list below.

      145 s   **192 s**   **115 s**

c) i) Name the **independent** variable in this experiment. ....

ii) Name the **dependent** variable in this experiment. ....

d) Suggest one way of obtaining results which are more **reliable**.

....

Q7 Jasmin uses the sodium thiosulfate and hydrochloric acid reaction to investigate the effect of varying the **concentration** of hydrochloric acid on the rate of reaction. She mixes the reagents together in a flask and times how long it takes for a cross placed under the flask to disappear.

She obtains these results:

Concentration of HCl (mol/dm^3)	2.00	1.75	1.50	1.25	1.00
Time taken for cross to disappear (s)	13	23	38	50	67

What conclusion can Yasmin draw from these results?

....

Top Tips: In precipitation reactions the quicker you stop being able to see through the reacting solutions the faster the reaction.

Chemistry 2(ii) — Rates of Reaction

Rate of Reaction Experiments

Q8 Hydrogen peroxide **decomposes** into water and oxygen.

a) What does 'decomposition' mean? ....

b) Complete the equation for the decomposition of hydrogen peroxide.

$$2H_2O_2 \rightleftharpoons \text{............} + O_2$$

Don't forget it needs to be balanced.

c) What is a good way to measure the speed of this reaction?
Circle the letter next to the correct answer.

    A   Weigh the amount of water produced

    B   Time how long the reaction takes to go cloudy

    C   Measure the volume of gas produced at regular time intervals

    D   Measure the temperature

d) Circle the correct words to complete the sentence.

We can **increase** / **decrease** the speed of this **displacement** / **decomposition**

reaction by using a catalyst like **magnesium oxide** / **manganese (IV) oxide**.

Q9 The decomposition of hydrogen peroxide can be used to investigate the effect of a **catalyst** on the rate of reaction. A student compared three different catalysts to see which was the most effective (increased the rate of reaction the most). He used a gas syringe to measure the amount of gas produced. Below is a graph of his results.

a) Label the y-axis (don't forget to include appropriate units).

b) The three catalysts used in this experiment were **manganese (IV) oxide**, **potato peel** and **blood**. Manganese (IV) oxide is the most effective catalyst for this reaction.

Using the graph, decide which curve (R, S, or T) represents the reaction using manganese (IV) oxide. Circle the correct letter.

    R   S   T

c) Explain your answer.

....

....

Chemistry 2(ii) — Rates of Reaction

Collision Theory

Q1 Draw lines to match up the changes with their effects.

- increasing the temperature
- decreasing the concentration
- adding a catalyst
- increasing the surface area

- provides a surface for particles to stick to and lowers activation energy
- makes the particles move faster, so they collide more often
- gives particles a bigger area of solid reactant to react with
- means fewer particles of reactant are present, so fewer collisions occur

Q2 Circle the correct words to complete the sentences.

a) If you heat up a reaction, you give the particles more **energy** / **surface area**.

b) This makes them move **faster** / **slower** so there is **more** / **less** chance of successful collisions.

c) So, increasing the temperature increases the **concentration** / **rate of reaction**.

Q3 Gases are always under **pressure**.

a) i) If you increase the pressure of a gas reaction, does the rate **increase** or **decrease**? ....

ii) Explain your answer.

....

....

b) In the boxes on the right draw two diagrams — one showing particles of two different gases at low pressure, the other showing the same two gases at high pressure.

low pressure   high pressure

Q4 Here are four statements about **surface area** and rates of reaction. Tick the appropriate boxes to show whether they are true or false.

True   False

a) Breaking a larger solid into smaller pieces decreases its surface area. ☐ ☐

b) A larger surface area will mean a faster rate of reaction. ☐ ☐

c) A larger surface area decreases the number of useful collisions. ☐ ☐

d) Powdered marble has a larger surface area than an equal mass of marble chips has. ☐ ☐

Q5 **Catalysts** affect particle collisions in a different way from changes in concentration and surface area. Do catalysts **increase** or **decrease** the number of **successful** collisions?

....

Chemistry 2(ii) — Rates of Reaction

Catalysts

Q1 To get a reaction to **start**, you have to give the particles some **energy**.

a) What is this energy called? Circle the correct answer.

potential energy   activation energy   chemical energy

b) The diagram opposite shows two reactions — one with a catalyst and one without. Which line shows the reaction **with** a catalyst, A or B? ....

c) On this diagram, draw and label arrows to show the activation energy for the reaction without a catalyst and the activation energy for the reaction with a catalyst.

Q2 Solid catalysts come in **different forms**. Two examples are **pellets** and **fine gauze**.

a) Name another form of solid catalyst. ....

b) Explain why solid catalysts are used in forms such as these.

....

c) How do catalysts help particles to react?

....

d) Suggest one potential problem associated with using catalysts in industrial processes.

....

Q3 Industrial catalysts are often **metals**.

You find them in the middle of the periodic table.

a) Which type of metals are commonly used? ....

b) Give an example of a catalyst and say which industrial process it is used in.

....

Q4 Modern cars have a '**catalytic converter**' in the exhaust system. It contains a platinum and rhodium **catalyst**. The catalyst converts highly toxic carbon monoxide (CO) in the exhaust gases, into non-toxic carbon dioxide (CO_2). Exhaust gases pass through the exhaust system very quickly.

Under normal conditions CO reacts with air to form CO_2, so why is a catalyst needed?

....

....

Chemistry 2(ii) — Rates of Reaction

Energy Transfer in Reactions

Q1 Circle the correct words in this paragraph about **exothermic** reactions.

Exothermic reactions **take in** / **give out** energy, usually in the form of **heat** / **sound**.

This is often shown by a **fall** / **rise** in **temperature** / **mass**.

Q2 Two examples of exothermic reactions are **burning fuels** and **neutralisation reactions**.

a) Write **B** for burning fuel or **N** for neutralisation reaction next to each of the following reactions.

☐ sulphuric acid + sodium hydroxide → sodium sulphate + water

☐ methane + oxygen → carbon dioxide + water

☐ potassium hydroxide + hydrochloric acid → potassium chloride + water

☐ ethanol + oxygen → carbon dioxide + water

b) Give another word for 'burning'. ....

c) Give **one** reaction in part a) which is also an oxidation reaction.

....

Q3 Fill in the missing words in this paragraph about **endothermic** reactions to make it correct.

Endothermic reactions .... energy, usually in the form of .... This is often shown by a .... in ....

Q4 Limestone (**calcium carbonate**, $CaCO_3$) decomposes when heated to form quicklime (calcium oxide, CaO) and carbon dioxide.

a) Write a balanced symbol equation for this reaction.

....

b) The reaction requires a large amount of heat.

i) Is it **exothermic** or **endothermic**? ....

ii) Explain your answer. ....

c) Decomposing 1 tonne (1000 kg) of $CaCO_3$ requires about 1 800 000 kJ of heat energy.

i) How much heat energy would be needed to make **1 kg** of $CaCO_3$ decompose?

....

ii) How much $CaCO_3$ could be decomposed by **90,000 kJ** of heat energy?

....

Chemistry 2(ii) — Rates of Reaction

Energy Transfer in Reactions

Q5 Sam did an experiment to investigate the **thermal decomposition** of **copper sulphate**. He wrote this about his investigation:

"When I heated up blue copper sulphate it steamed and went white. After it cooled down I dropped a little water on it and it got really hot and turned blue again".

Answer these questions about Sam's observations:

a) Which part of Sam's experiment was exothermic? ....

b) Which part of Sam's experiment was endothermic? ....

c) Is blue copper sulphate **anhydrous** or **hydrated**? Circle the correct answer.

anhydrous

hydrated

Anhydrous means without water and hydrated means containing water.

d) Below is the equation for the reaction.
On the dotted lines write what **colour** the copper sulphate is on each side of the equation.

$$CuSO_4 \cdot 5H_2O \rightleftharpoons CuSO_4 + 5H_2O$$

....

Q6 Here are some practical uses of chemical reactions. Decide whether each reaction is endothermic or exothermic. In the box, put **N** for endothermic and **X** for exothermic.

a) A camping stove burns methylated spirit to heat a pan of beans. ☐

b) Special chemical cool packs are used by athletes to treat injuries. They are placed on the skin and draw heat away from the injury. ☐

c) Self-heating cans of coffee contain chemicals in the base. When the chemicals are combined they produce heat which warms the can. ☐

d) Baking powder is used to make cakes rise. When it's heated in the oven it thermally decomposes to produce a gas. ☐

Top Tips: Anything that takes heat in is endothermic. Endothermic reactions are pretty rare in everyday life but they do occur, think about cooking eggs and using baking powder.

Chemistry 2(ii) — Rates of Reaction

Reversible Reactions

Q1 Use words from the list below to complete the following sentences about **reversible reactions**.

escape   reactants   catalysts   closed   products   react   balance

a) In a reversible reaction, the .... of the reaction can themselves .... to give the original ....

b) In an equilibrium, the amounts of reactants and products reach a ....

c) To reach equilibrium the reaction must happen in a .... system, where products and reactants can't ....

Q2 Look at this diagram of a **reversible reaction**.

The reaction going from left to right is called the forward reaction. The reaction going from right to left is called the backward reaction.

a) For the forward reaction:
  i) give the reactant(s) ....
  ii) give the product(s) ....

b) i) Here are two labels:

   | X product splits up |
   | Y reactants combine |

   Which of these labels goes in position 1 — X or Y? ....

  ii) Which label goes in position 2 — X or Y? ....

c) Write the equation for the reversible reaction. ....

d) Complete the sentence by circling the correct phrase.

In a dynamic equilibrium, the forward and backward reactions are happening
at different rates / at zero rate / at the same rate.

Q3 Which of these statements about reversible reactions are **true** and which are **false**?

		True	False
a)	The position of equilibrium depends on the reaction conditions.	☐	☐
b)	Upon reaching a dynamic equilibrium, the reactions stop taking place.	☐	☐
c)	You can move the position of equilibrium to get more product.	☐	☐
d)	At equilibrium there will always be equal quantities of products and reactants.	☐	☐

Chemistry 2(ii) — Rates of Reaction

Reversible Reactions

Q4 Substances A and B react to produce substances C and D in a reversible reaction.

$$2A_{(g)} + B_{(g)} \rightleftharpoons 2C_{(g)} + D_{(g)}$$

a) Give two reaction conditions which affect the **position of equilibrium**.

1. ....
2. ....

b) The forward reaction is **exothermic**. Does the backward reaction give out or take in heat? Explain your answer.

....

c) If the **temperature** is raised, which reaction will increase, the forward or the backward reaction?

....

d) Explain why changing the temperature of a reversible reaction always affects the position of equilibrium.

....

e) What effect will changing the **pressure** have on the position of equilibrium of this reaction? Explain your answer.

This reaction has equal numbers of molecules on each side of the reaction.

....

Q5 a) In this reaction:

$$2SO_{2(g)} + O_{2(g)} \rightleftharpoons 2SO_{3(g)}$$

i) Which reaction, forward or backward, is accompanied by a **decrease** in volume? Explain your answer.

....

ii) How will increasing the pressure affect the position of equilibrium in this reaction?

....

b) What does adding a catalyst to a reversible reaction do? Circle the letter next to the correct answer.

A It moves the equilibrium position towards the products.

B It makes the reaction achieve equilibrium more quickly.

C It moves the equilibrium position towards the reactants.

D It causes a decrease in pressure.

c) What happens to the amount of product when you use a catalyst?

....

Chemistry 2(ii) — Rates of Reaction

The Haber Process

Q1 The Haber process is used to make **ammonia**.

a) The equation for the reaction is

$$N_2(g) + 3H_2(g) \rightleftharpoons 2NH_3(g)$$

   i) Name the reactants in the forward reaction ....

   ii) Which side of the equation has more molecules? ....

b) Name a **useful substance** that can be made from ammonia.

   ....

Q2 The **industrial conditions** for the Haber process are carefully chosen.

a) What conditions are used? Tick one box.

   ☐ 1000 atmospheres, 450 °C   ☐ 200 atmospheres, 1000 °C   ☐ 450 atmospheres, 200 °C   ☐ 200 atmospheres, 450 °C

b) Give two reasons why the pressure used is chosen.

   1. ....

   2. ....

Q3 In the Haber process reaction, the forward reaction is **exothermic**.

a) What effect will raising the temperature have on the **amount** of ammonia formed?

   ....

b) Explain why a high temperature is used industrially.

   ....

c) What happens to the leftover nitrogen and hydrogen? ....

Q4 The Haber process uses an **iron catalyst**.

a) What effect does this have on the % yield? ....

b) Iron catalysts are relatively cheap. What effect does using one have on the **cost** of producing the ammonia? Explain your answer.

   ....

   ....

Top Tips: Changing the conditions in a reversible reaction to get more product sounds great, but don't forget that these conditions might be too difficult or expensive for factories to produce, or they might mean a reaction that's too slow to be profitable.

Chemistry 2(ii) — Rates of Reaction

Mixed Questions — Chemistry 2(ii)

Q1 Several factors affect **how quickly** chemical reactions occur.

a) Name four things that can **increase** the rate of a reaction.

....

....

....

b) What are the three main **experimental methods** used to measure reaction rates?

....

....

....

Q2 The graph shows the results from an experiment using magnesium and dilute hydrochloric acid. The **change in mass** of the reactants was measured using a balance.

a) Which reaction was **faster**, P or Q?

....

b) Which reaction used the **most** reactants, P, Q or R?

....

c) The reaction produces a **gas**. Which other experimental method could you have used to measure the rate of reaction?

....

Q3 Indicate whether each of the following statements is **true** or **false** by ticking the correct box.

 True False

a) When measuring the change in mass of a reaction, the quicker the reading on the balance drops, the faster the reaction. ☐ ☐

b) Using a gas syringe to measure the volume of gas given off is usually quite accurate. ☐ ☐

c) An explosion is an example of a slow reaction. ☐ ☐

d) On a rate of reaction graph the line with the steepest slope shows the fastest rate of reaction. ☐ ☐

e) If the same amount of reactants are used the same amount of product will be produced, regardless of the rate of reaction. ☐ ☐

Chemistry 2(ii) — Rates of Reaction

Mixed Questions — Chemistry 2(ii)

Q4 When a chemical reaction occurs, **energy** is taken in or given out to the surroundings.

   a) Define 'exothermic'.
   ....

   b) Susan burned some wood. Was the reaction endothermic or exothermic? ....

   c) i) Are **thermal decomposition** reactions endothermic or exothermic? ....

   ii) Give two examples of substances that thermally decompose.
   ....

   d) In a particular reversible reaction the forward reaction is endothermic.
   Draw a line to match each sentence beginning to its correct ending.

   | If you increase the temperature... | | you increase the reverse reaction. |
   | If you decrease the temperature... | | you increase the forward reaction. |

Q5 The Haber process is a **reversible reaction**.

   a) Write a **balanced symbol equation** for the reaction. ....

   b) The Haber process uses an **iron catalyst**.

   i) Complete the paragraph about catalysts by circling the correct words.

   > Some catalysts give reacting particles a surface to stick to. They **increase / decrease** the number of successful collisions by **lowering / raising** the activation energy of a reaction. Catalysts are used in industry to save money because they often allow a **lower / higher** temperature to be used.

   ii) Catalysts are often used in a **powdered** form. Explain why.
   ....
   ....

   c) The Haber process is carried out at a pressure of 200 atmospheres.

   i) What effect does **pressure** have on the **number of collisions** in a reaction?
   ....

   ii) Does raising the pressure **increase** or **decrease** the rate of the forward reaction? ....

   iii) Explain why. ....

   d) The forward reaction of the Haber process is **exothermic**. If you **increase** the temperature will you increase or decrease the amount of ammonia produced?
   Circle the correct answer: increase   decrease

Chemistry 2(ii) — Rates of Reaction

Chemistry 2(iii) — Using Ions in Solution

Acids and Alkalis

Q1 a) Complete the equation below for the reaction between an acid and a base.

acid + base → .... + ...

b) Circle the correct term for this kind of reaction.

decomposition   oxidation   neutralisation

c) Which of the following ions:

$H^+(aq)$ $OH^-(aq)$ $Cl^-(aq)$ $Na^+(aq)$

i) react with each other to form water? ....

ii) is present in an acidic solution? ....

iii) is present in an alkaline solution? ....

iv) would combine to form the salt sodium chloride? ....

v) would be present in a solution with a pH of 10? ....

vi) would be found in lemon juice? ....

Q2 Joey wanted to test whether some antacid tablets really do **neutralise acid**.

He added a tablet to some hydrochloric acid, stirred it until it dissolved and tested the pH of the solution. Further tests were carried out after dissolving a second, third and fourth tablet. His results are shown in the table below.

Number of Tablets	pH
0	1
1	2
2	3
3	7
4	9

a) i) Plot a graph of the results.

ii) Describe how the pH changes when antacid tablets are added to the acid.

....

iii) How many tablets were needed to neutralise the acid?

....

b) Joey tested another brand of tablets and found that **two** tablets neutralised the same volume of acid. On the graph, sketch the results you might expect for these tablets.

Acids and Alkalis

Q3 a) Circle the correct words to complete the sentences.

    i) A soluble base is called an **acid** / **alkali**.

    ii) Alkalis form **H⁺** / **OH⁻** ions in water.

    iii) Acids form **H⁺** / **OH⁻** ions in water.

b) Fill in the blanks using some of the words below.

| increases | acidic | lime | water | acid | alkali | neutralises | decreases |

When lime is added to acidic soil it .... the acid and .... the pH of the soil. Indigestion tablets contain a base which neutralises the excess .... in the stomach. Pollution caused by sulfur dioxide makes lakes .... which can kill the organisms that live there, so .... is added to lakes to neutralise the acid.

Q4 Ants' stings hurt because of the **formic acid** they release. The pH measurements of some household substances are given in the table.

SUBSTANCE	pH
lemon juice	4
baking soda	9
caustic soda	14
soap powder	11

    a) Describe how you could test the formic acid to find its pH value.

    ....

    ....

    b) Suggest a substance from the list that could be used to relieve the discomfort of an ant sting. Explain your answer.

    ....

    ....

    c) Explain why universal indicator only gives an **estimate** of the pH.

    ....

    ....

Q5 Complete the following sentences.

    a) Solutions which are not acidic or alkaline are said to be ....

    b) Universal indicator is a combination of different coloured ....

    c) If a substance is neutral it has a pH of ....

    d) Indigestion occurs when the stomach produces too much ....

Chemistry 2(iii) — Using Ions in Solution

Acids Reacting with Metals

Q1 The diagram below shows **aluminium** reacting with **sulfuric acid**.

a) Label the diagram with the names of the chemicals.

b) Complete the word equation for this reaction:
   aluminium + ... → **aluminium sulfate** + ...

c) Write a balanced symbol equation for this reaction.
   ....

   The formula of aluminium sulfate is $Al_2(SO_4)_3$.

d) Zinc also reacts with sulfuric acid. Give the word equation for this reaction.
   ....

e) Write a balanced symbol equation for the reaction between:

   i) Magnesium and hydrochloric acid ....

   ii) Calcium and nitric acid ....

Q2 The table shows what happens when different **metals** react with **hydrochloric acid**.

Metal	A	B	C	D
Observations	gas bubbles formed vigorously	no gas bubbles formed	gas bubbles form slowly	gas bubbles form steadily
	metal dissolved quickly	metal unaffected by the acid	most of the metal remained after 5 min	most of the metal dissolved after 5 min

a) Which is the **most** reactive metal? ....

b) Which metal(s) are **less** reactive than hydrogen? ....

c) Which metal(s) are **more** reactive than hydrogen? ....

d) The metals used in this experiment were magnesium, zinc, iron and copper. Match each of these metals to the correct letter from the table.

   A ....

   B ....

   C ....

   D ....

   Look at the reactivity series to help you.

Chemistry 2(iii) — Using Ions in Solution

Acids Reacting with Metals

Q3 Rhiannon is planning an experiment to investigate the rate of reaction between magnesium and different **concentrations** of hydrochloric acid.

a) How could she measure the rate of the reaction?

....

b) What is the **independent variable** in her experiment?

....

c) Give two variables that she will need to keep the **same** in her experiment.

....

Q4 Fill in the blanks using some of the words given below.

reactive   silver   nitric   more   hydrogen   less   chlorides
sulfuric   carbon dioxide   non-metals   nitrates   metals

Acids react with most .... to form salts and .... gas. Metals like copper and .... which are less .... than hydrogen don't react with acids. The .... reactive the metal, the more vigorously the bubbles of gas form. Hydrochloric acid forms .... and .... acid produces sulfates. However, the reactions of metals with .... acid don't follow this simple pattern.

Q5 a) Write out the **balanced** versions of the following equations.

i) $Ca + HCl \rightarrow CaCl_2 + H_2$ ....

ii) $Na + HCl \rightarrow NaCl + H_2$ ....

iii) $Li + H_2SO_4 \rightarrow Li_2SO_4 + H_2$ ....

b) Hydrobromic acid reacts with magnesium as shown in the equation below to form a bromide salt and hydrogen.

$$Mg + 2HBr \rightarrow MgBr_2 + H_2$$

i) Name the salt formed in this reaction. ....

ii) Write a balanced symbol equation for the reaction between aluminium and hydrobromic acid. (The formula of aluminium bromide is $AlBr_3$.)

....

Chemistry 2(iii) — Using Ions in Solution

Oxides, Hydroxides and Ammonia

Q1 Fill in the blanks to complete the word equations for **acids** reacting with **metal oxides** and **metal hydroxides**.

a) hydrochloric acid + lead oxide → .... chloride + water

b) nitric acid + copper hydroxide → copper .... + water

c) sulfuric acid + zinc oxide → zinc sulfate + ...

d) hydrochloric acid + ... oxide → nickel .... + ...

e) .... acid + copper oxide → .... nitrate + ...

f) sulfuric acid + ... hydroxide → sodium .... + ...

Q2 a) Put a tick in the box next to any of the sentences below which are **true**.

Alkalis are bases which don't dissolve in water. ☐

Acids react with metal oxides to form a salt and water. ☐

Hydrogen gas is formed when an acid reacts with an alkali. ☐

Salts and water are formed when acids react with metal hydroxides. ☐

Ammonia solution is alkaline. ☐

Calcium hydroxide is an acid that dissolves in water. ☐

b) Use the formulas below to write **symbol equations** for two acid/base reactions.

H_2SO_4 H_2O CuO $NaCl$ HCl $NaOH$
   H_2O $CuSO_4$

....

....

Q3 Name two substances which would react to make each of the following **salts**.

a) Potassium sulfate ....

b) Ammonium chloride ....

c) Silver nitrate ....

Chemistry 2(iii) — Using Ions in Solution

Oxides, Hydroxides and Ammonia

Q4 Ammonia can be neutralised by nitric acid to form a salt.

a) Underline the correct formula for ammonia below.

NH_4NO_3 NH_4Cl NH_3 NH_2 NH_4

b) Fill in the blanks in the passage below using some of the words from the list.

proteins   solid   gas   fertilisers   acidic   nitrogen   liquid   salts   alkaline

> Ammonia is a .... at room temperature which dissolves in water to form an .... solution. Ammonia contains .... which plants need to produce ...., so it is used to make ammonium .... which are widely used as ....

c) Write down the word equation for making **ammonium nitrate**.

....

d) Why is ammonium nitrate a particularly good fertiliser?

....

e) How is this neutralisation reaction different from most neutralisation reactions?

....

Q5 a) Complete the following equations.

i) $H_2SO_4(aq)$ + ... → $CuSO_4(aq)$ + $H_2O(l)$

ii) $2HNO_3(aq)$ + $MgO(s)$ → $Mg(NO_3)_2(aq)$ + ...

iii) .... + $KOH(aq)$ → $KCl(aq)$ + $H_2O(l)$

iv) $2HCl(aq)$ + ... → $ZnCl_2(aq)$ + $H_2O(l)$

v) $H_2SO_4(aq)$ + $2NaOH(aq)$ → .... + ...

b) **Balance** the following acid/base reactions.

i) $NaOH$ + H_2SO_4 → Na_2SO_4 + H_2O

ii) $Mg(OH)_2$ + HNO_3 → $Mg(NO_3)_2$ + H_2O

iii) NH_3 + H_2SO_4 → $(NH_4)_2SO_4$

Chemistry 2(iii) — Using Ions in Solution

Making Salts

Q1 Complete the following sentences by circling the correct word from each pair.

a) Most chlorides, sulfates and nitrates are **soluble** / **insoluble** in water.

b) Most oxides, hydroxides and carbonates are **soluble** / **insoluble** in water.

c) Soluble salts can be made by reacting acids with **soluble** / **insoluble** bases until they are just **neutralised** / **displaced**.

d) Insoluble salts are made by **precipitation** / **electrolysis**.

e) Salts can be made by displacement, where a **more** / **less** reactive metal is put into a salt solution of a **more** / **less** reactive metal.

Care of Animals Rule No. 57: Never pour salt in a rabbit's eyes.

Q2 **A**, **B**, **C** and **D** are symbol equations for reactions in which **salts** are formed.

A $CuO(s) + H_2SO_4(aq) \rightarrow CuSO_4(aq) + H_2O(l)$

B $2NaOH(aq) + H_2SO_4(aq) \rightarrow Na_2SO_4(aq) + 2H_2O(l)$

C $Zn(s) + 2AgNO_3(aq) \rightarrow Zn(NO_3)_2(aq) + 2Ag(s)$

D $Pb(NO_3)_2(aq) + H_2SO_4(aq) \rightarrow PbSO_4(s) + 2HNO_3(aq)$

Which equation (A, B, C or D) refers to the formation of a salt:

a) in an acid/alkali reaction. ....   b) by precipitation. ....

c) from an insoluble base. ....   d) by displacement. ....

Q3 A piece of **magnesium** is dropped into a solution of **copper sulfate**.

a) Explain why the piece of magnesium becomes coated in an **orange-coloured** substance.

....

....

b) A new salt is formed during this experiment. Name this salt.

....

c) Once all the the magnesium is coated with the orange substance, the reaction stops. Explain why.

....

....

d) What type of reaction is this? Circle your answer.   **displacement**   **neutralisation**   **electrolysis**

Chemistry 2(iii) — Using Ions in Solution

Making Salts

Q4 **Silver chloride** is an insoluble salt which is formed as a **precipitate** when silver nitrate and sodium chloride solutions are mixed together.

a) Complete the word equation for the reaction.

.... + ... → silver chloride + ...

b) After mixing the solutions to produce a precipitate, what further steps are needed to produce a dry sample of silver chloride?

....

....

Q5 **Nickel sulfate** (a soluble salt) was made by adding insoluble **nickel carbonate** to **sulfuric acid** until no further reaction occurred.

a) What piece of apparatus is being used to add the nickel carbonate in the diagram?

....

b) State two observations that would tell you that the reaction was complete.

1. ....

2. ....

Once the reaction was complete, the excess nickel carbonate was separated from the nickel sulfate solution using the apparatus shown.

c) Label the diagram which shows the separation process.

....

....

....

d) What is this method of separation called?

....

e) Describe how you could produce a solid sample of nickel sulfate from nickel sulfate solution.

....

....

Chemistry 2(iii) — Using Ions in Solution

Electrolysis and the Half-Equations

Q1 **Lead bromide** is an ionic substance. It doesn't easily dissolve in water.

a) How could lead bromide be made into a liquid for electrolysis?

....

b) Write **balanced** half-equations for the processes that occur at the cathode and anode during the electrolysis of lead bromide.

Remember, when bromide ions lose electrons they pair up to become bromine molecules (Br_2).

Cathode: ....

Anode: ....

Q2 The diagram below shows the electrolysis of a **salt solution**.

a) Identify the ions and molecules labelled A, B, C and D on the diagram. Choose from the options in the box below.

Na^+	H^+	Cl_2	H_2
Cl^-		Na_2	H_2O

A ....   B ....

C ....   D ....

b) Write **balanced** half-equations for the processes that occur during the electrolysis of this salt solution.

Make sure the charges balance.

Cathode: ....

Anode: ....

Q3 After electrolysing a salt solution, Englebert noticed that the laboratory had a similar smell to his local **swimming pool**.

a) Suggest why this was. ....

....

b) Explain why this could be a safety issue. ....

c) Suggest what could be done in future to make this experiment safer.

....

Q4 Explain why a substance needs to be either in a **solution** or **molten** for electrolysis to work.

....

Top Tips: Half-equations just show what's going on at the cathode and anode in terms of electrons — a positive ion gains electrons (and a negative ion loses electrons) to make neutral atoms.

Chemistry 2(iii) — Using Ions in Solution

Electrolysis of Salt Water

Q1 Describe simple **lab tests** for the following products of the electrolysis of brine.

a) hydrogen

....

....

b) chlorine

....

Q2 Harry runs a little **brine electrolysis** business from his garden shed. He keeps a record of all the different **industries** that he sells his products to.

HARRY'S BRINE PRODUCTS LTD. — FINAL USES

Pie chart segments:
- disinfectants 8%
- ceramics 2%
- other 11%
- soap x%
- paper pulp 8%
- other 11%
- margarine 14%
- other 5%
- insecticide 6%
- plastics 21%

Legend: chlorine, hydrogen, sodium hydroxide

a) Which brine product, **hydrogen**, **chlorine** or **sodium hydroxide**, does Harry sell the most of?

....

b) What percentage of Harry's products are used to manufacture **soap**?

....

c) Suggest one other use of sodium hydroxide that is not mentioned on the chart above.

....

d) Which **industry** uses the biggest proportion of Harry's products?

....

Chemistry 2(iii) — Using Ions in Solution

Electrolysis of Salt Water

Q3 Use the words in the box below to complete the paragraph about the electrolysis of **brine**.

| chlorine | cathode | ammonia | sodium hydroxide | concentrated |
| soap | margarine | ceramics | plastics | disinfectant |

During the electrolysis, ... brine is split into three useful products. At the anode .... gas is produced. This can be used as a .... in swimming pools and also in the manufacture of .... At the .... hydrogen gas is given off. This can be used in the manufacture of .... and .... is left in solution. This strong alkali is used to make .... and ....

Q4 Imagine it is your job to find a location to carry out the electrolysis of brine on an **industrial scale** (coincidentally, that was always my dream job when I was at school). Describe the **ideal location** of your industrial plant.

Think about what you need for the process, and the major costs associated with it.

Q5 Two gases, hydrogen and chlorine, are produced during the electrolysis of brine in the lab. Explain how the two gases can be **collected separately**.

Chemistry 2(iii) — Using Ions in Solution

Purifying Copper by Electrolysis

Q1 Write **half-equations** for the purification of copper by electrolysis.

Cathode: ....

Anode: ....

Q2 During the electrolytic purification of copper, the **impure sludge** simply falls to the bottom. It does **not** follow the copper ions to the cathode. Why do you think this is?

....

....

The copper ions that leave the anode are positively charged.

Q3 a) How is copper extracted from **copper ore** found in the ground?

....

b) Why might this extracted copper need to be purified?

....

c) What is used as the **anode** during copper purification by electrolysis?

....

d) Explain why pure copper ends up at the **cathode** during electrolysis.

....

....

Q4 Silver can be purified in the same way as copper. Write **half-equations** for the processes that takes place at the anode and the cathode.

Silver forms 1^+ ions.

Cathode: ....

Anode: ....

Q5 Why would it **not** be a good idea to carry out the electrolysis of **copper** in an electrolyte that contained **zinc** ions instead of copper ions. Tick the correct box.

The zinc ions will not conduct an electrical current.	☐
The copper produced will have zinc impurities in it.	☐
A poisonous gas would be produced.	☐
The zinc and copper ions will react with each other.	☐

Chemistry 2(iii) — Using Ions in Solution

Mixed Questions — Chemistry 2(iii)

Q1 The diagram shows the **pH scale**.

| 1 | 2 | 3 | 4 | 5 | 6 | 7 | 8 | 9 | 10 | 11 | 12 | 13 |

↑ black coffee (at 5) ↑ milk of magnesia (at 10)

a) The pH values of black coffee and milk of magnesia are marked on the diagram.

   i) Is black coffee neutral, acidic or alkaline? ....

   ii) Is milk of magnesia neutral, acidic or alkaline? ....

b) Indigestion is caused by the production of excess acid in the stomach. Milk of magnesia is used as an indigestion remedy. It contains a suspension of magnesium hydroxide, $Mg(OH)_2$. Explain how milk of magnesia can help with indigestion.

....

....

Q2 Rose added a piece of **magnesium** to some **HCl** and watched what happened.

a) Complete and **balance** the chemical equation for the reaction.

   .... Mg + ... HCl → .... + ...

b) Explain how the **pH** would change as the magnesium was added.

....

c) What is the name of the salt formed by magnesium and **sulfuric acid**? ....

Q3 Some solid **magnesium oxide** was added to **HCl** solution in a test tube. The reactants and the products are shown, but the equation is **not** balanced.

   $MgO\,(s) + HCl\,(aq) \rightarrow D\,(aq) + H_2O\,(l)$

a) i) Give the chemical formula of substance **D**? ....

   ii) What would be observed as the reaction **proceeded**?

....

b) When solid magnesium oxide was added to a substance **S**, magnesium sulfate and water were formed. Identify S by name or formula. ....

c) Are most oxides **soluble** or **insoluble** in water? ....

Q4 Why is it difficult to make a salt by neutralisation if both the salt and the base are **soluble**?

....

....

....

Chemistry 2(iii) — Using Ions in Solution

Mixed Questions — Chemistry 2(iii)

Q5 Aluminium is extracted from its ore by **electrolysis**.

a) The aluminium ions are attracted to the **negative** electrode.

  i) Explain what happens to the aluminium ions at the negative electrode.

  ....

  ....

  ii) Complete a balanced half-equation for the reaction. Al^{3+} + ... → ....

b) The **oxygen** ions are attracted to the **positive** electrode.
Complete a balanced half-equation for the reaction. $2O^{2-}$ → .... + ...

Q6 a) Label the diagram showing the electrolysis of a solution of **sodium chloride**. Use the following labels:

- chloride ions
- chlorine hydrogen
- diaphragm
- sodium ions
- sodium hydroxide solution

B .... gas given off.

C .... gas given off.

D .... and
E .... in solution.

A ....

F ....

b) Give one **use** for each of the products of this reaction.

Chlorine .... Hydrogen ....

Sodium hydroxide ....

Q7 Copper can be **purified** by electrolysis.

a) Why does copper sometimes need to be purified?

....

....

b) Copper metal in the impure anode becomes copper ions. Why do they travel towards the **cathode**?

....

c) Explain what happens when the copper ions reach the cathode.

....

Chemistry 2(iii) — Using Ions in Solution

History of the Periodic Table

Q1 Complete the sentences below.

a) In the modern periodic table, the elements are ordered according to their ....

b) Before this, the known elements were arranged in order according to their ....

Q2 Say whether the following statements about **Mendeleev's** Table of Elements are **true** or **false**.

a) Mendeleev left gaps in the table for undiscovered elements. ....

b) Mendeleev arranged the elements in order of increasing atomic number. ....

c) Mendeleev was able to predict the properties of undiscovered elements. ....

d) Elements with similar properties appeared in the same rows. ....

Q3 When **Newlands** arranged the known elements in order of **atomic mass** in 1864, the first three rows were as shown.

1						2
H	Li	Be	B	C	N	O
F	Na	Mg	Al	Si	P	S
Cl	K	Ca	Cr	Ti	Mn	Fe

a) In which of the two highlighted groups do the elements have similar properties? ....

b) This arrangement of elements was known as 'Newlands' Octaves'. Why did Newlands arrange the elements in rows of seven?

....

c) Why didn't helium and neon appear in Newlands' table?

....

Q4 Mendeleev left **gaps** in his Table of Elements to keep elements with similar properties in the same groups. He predicted that elements would eventually be discovered to fill the gaps. For example, he predicted the discovery of an element that would fill a gap in his Group 4 and called it '**ekasilicon**'.

Element	Density g/cm³
carbon	2.27
silicon	2.33
'ekasilicon'	
tin	7.29
lead	11.34

The table shows the **densities** of known elements in this group.

a) 'Ekasilicon' was eventually discovered and given another name. Use the information in the table to decide which of the elements below is 'ekasilicon'. Circle your choice.

palladium, 12.02 g/cm³   germanium, 5.32 g/cm³   beryllium, 1.85 g/cm³   copper, 8.93 g/cm³

b) i) What did Mendeleev's arrangement have **in common** with Newlands' earlier attempt?

....

....

ii) What was the main **difference** between their approaches?

....

The Modern Periodic Table

Q1 The **electron arrangements** of some atoms are shown below.

a) In which of these atoms is the outermost electron **furthest** from the nucleus? ....

b) In which of these atoms is the outermost electron **least shielded** from the nucleus? ....

c) In which of these atoms is the outermost electron **most easily lost**? ....

d) Which of these atoms is the **most** reactive? ....

e) Which of these atoms is the **least** reactive? ....

Q2 The **periodic table** below contains the symbols of some elements in their correct places.

a) Which three elements above have the most similar chemical properties? ....

b) Give the chemical symbols of the two most unreactive elements shown above. ....

c) Which element shown above has a higher atomic number than Rb? ....

Q3 A periodic table is shown with **electron configurations** for some of the elements.

a) How does the number of electrons in the outer shell of each atom relate to the **group** it is in?

....

b) Write down the electron configurations for:

magnesium .... oxygen .... sulfur ....

c) Is oxygen likely to be more or less reactive than sulfur? Explain your answer.

....
....

Chemistry 3(i) — Elements, Acids and Water

The Modern Periodic Table

Q4 The table shows the electron configurations for some **Group I** and **Group VII** elements.

Group I	Electron Configuration	Group VII	Electron Configuration
Li	2, 1	F	2, 7
Na	2, 8, 1	Cl	2, 8, 7
K	2, 8, 8, 1	Br	2, 8, 18, 7

It's an element, my dear Watson.

a) What term is used for the reduced nuclear attraction for outer electrons, caused by inner electrons?

....

b) i) Why do potassium atoms lose their outer electron more easily than lithium atoms?

....

....

ii) Does this make potassium more or less reactive than lithium?

....

c) i) Explain why fluorine atoms attract electrons more strongly than bromine atoms.

....

....

ii) Explain the trend in the reactivities of the Group VII elements in terms of nuclear attraction.

....

....

Q5 **Potassium** has an atomic number of **19**.

a) In the space below, draw a diagram to show the electron arrangement for potassium.

Have a look at the diagrams in Q1 on the last page — that's the type of thing you need.

b) In which group of the periodic table would you expect to find potassium?

....

c) There are two elements in the same group as potassium that have smaller atomic numbers. Would you expect these elements to be more or less reactive than potassium? Explain your answer.

....

....

Chemistry 3(i) — Elements, Acids and Water

Group I — The Alkali Metals

Q1 Sodium, potassium and lithium are all alkali metals.

Put these three alkali metals in order of increasing reactivity.

least reactive .... most reactive

Q2 Indicate whether the statements below about the alkali metals are **true** or **false**.

True False
a) They readily gain electrons to form 1⁺ ions. ☐ ☐
b) They form covalent compounds by sharing electrons. ☐ ☐
c) They are stored in oil to stop them reacting with oxygen and water in the air. ☐ ☐
d) Their atoms all have a single electron in the outer shell. ☐ ☐

Q3 Circle the correct word(s) from each pair to complete the passage below.

Sodium is a **soft** / **hard** metal with a low melting point. It reacts vigorously with water producing **sodium dioxide** / **sodium hydroxide** and **hydrogen** / **oxygen** gas. When it reacts, it loses its outermost **proton** / **electron**, forming an ion with a **positive** / **negative** charge.

Q4 The table shows the **melting points** of some Group I metals.

Element	MELTING PT (°C)
Li	181
Na	98
K	63
Rb	39
Cs	28

a) What is unusual about the **melting points** of these metals?

....

b) Describe the **trend** in the melting point as you move down this group.

....

c) Complete the following sentences which describe other trends seen in the Group I elements:

  i) As you move **down** Group I, the **size** of the atoms ....

  ii) As you move **up** Group I, the **density** of the atoms ....

Q5 Archibald put a piece of **lithium** into a beaker of water.

a) Explain why the lithium floated on top of the water.

....

b) After the reaction had finished, Archibald tested the water with universal indicator. What colour change would he see, and why?

....

....

c) Write a **balanced symbol equation** for the reaction. ....

Chemistry 3(i) — Elements, Acids and Water

Group VII — The Halogens

Q1 Draw lines to match each halogen to its **description**.

HALOGEN
bromine
chlorine
fluorine
iodine

DESCRIPTION
yellow gas
grey solid
red-brown liquid
green-yellow gas

Hubba hubba

Q2 Say whether these statements are **true** or **false**. True False

a) Chlorine gas is made up of molecules which each contain three chlorine atoms.

b) Halogens combine with other non-metals to form molecules with covalent bonding.

c) Chlorine reacts with carbon to form an ionic compound.

d) The melting points of the halogens increase down the group.

Q3 Draw lines to match the phrases and complete the sentences.

The halogens exist as molecules ...   ... forming ionic salts.

A more reactive halogen ...   ... decreases as you move down the group.

The halogens react with most metals ...   ... which are pairs of atoms.

The reactivity of the halogens ...   ... will displace a less reactive one.

Q4 **Iron** can be reacted with **bromine** in a fume cupboard. An **orange solid** forms on the sides of the test tube.

a) Why is a fume cupboard necessary to carry out this reaction?

....

b) Name the compound formed. ....

c) What type of bonding is present in this compound? ....

Q5 Equal volumes of **bromine water** were added to two test tubes, each containing a different **potassium halide solution**. The results are shown in the table.

SOLUTION	RESULT
potassium chloride	no change
potassium iodide	solution changed colour

a) Explain these results.

....

....

b) Write a **balanced symbol equation** (including state symbols) for the reaction in the iodide solution.

....

Chemistry 3(i) — Elements, Acids and Water

Transition Elements

Q1 Complete the passage below by circling the correct word(s) from each pair.

Most metals are in the transition block found **at the left / in the middle** of the periodic table. The transition metals are usually **reactive / unreactive** with oxygen and water. They generally have high **densities / volatility** and **low / high** melting points. They are **good / poor** conductors of heat and electricity. Their compounds are **coloured / shiny** and, like the metals themselves, are effective **fuels / catalysts** in many reactions.

Q2 Answer the questions below about **transition metals**. (Underline your answer in each part.)

a) Which one of the following properties applies to **all metals**?

high density   good conductivity   high melting point   high tensile strength

b) Which one of the following properties applies to **all transition metals**?

low density   low melting point   poor conductivity   shiny appearance

c) Which electron arrangement below is that of a transition metal?

2, 8, 8, 2   2, 8, 1   2, 8, 16, 2   2, 8, 8

Q3 Transition metals and their compounds often make good catalysts.

a) Draw lines to match the metals and compounds below to the reactions they catalyse.

iron   converting natural oils into fats

nickel   ammonia production

manganese(IV) oxide   decomposition of hydrogen peroxide

b) Give the electron arrangements of the following transition metals. (The first one's been done for you.)

Titanium   2, 8, 10, 2

i) Iron ....

ii) Vanadium ....

iii) Nickel ....

HINT: the atomic number is the same as the total number of electrons in an atom.

c) Transition metals often form more than one ion. Write down two different ions formed by:

i) Iron ....   ii) Copper ....   iii) Chromium ....

Chemistry 3(i) — Elements, Acids and Water

Transition Elements

Q4 'Chemical gardens' can be made by sprinkling **transition metal salts** into **sodium silicate solution**. Transition metal silicate crystals grow upwards as shown.

a) Suggest three colours that you would be likely to see in the garden if iron(II) sulfate, iron(III) chloride and copper sulfate crystals are used.

....

b) Cobalt(II) chloride produces pink cobalt silicate crystals.

i) What is the electron configuration of a cobalt atom? ....

ii) Which cobalt ion is present in cobalt(II) chloride? ....

iii) Complete the word equation for the reaction which forms cobalt silicate crystals.

sodium silicate + cobalt chloride → .... + ...

Q5 Read the description of **metal X** and answer the questions that follow.

'Metal X is found in the block of elements between groups II and III in the periodic table. It has a melting point of 1860 °C and a density of 7.2 g/cm³. The metal is used to provide the attractive shiny coating on motorbikes and bathroom taps. The metal forms two coloured chlorides, XCl_2 (blue) and XCl_3 (green).'

Identify six pieces of evidence in the passage which suggest that metal X is a transition metal.

1. ....

2. ....

3. ....

4. ....

5. ....

6. ....

Top Tips:
Most of the first 10 transition metals have two electrons in the 4th energy level. Chromium and copper are a little bit different — they only have one electron in the 4th energy level.

Chemistry 3(i) — Elements, Acids and Water

Acids and Alkalis

Q1 Some particles found in acids and alkalis are: $H^+(aq)$ $H_2O(l)$ $OH^-(aq)$

   a) Which particle would make a solution **acidic**? ....

   b) Which particle would make a solution **alkaline**? ....

   c) Which particle is a 'hydrated proton'? ....

Q2 **Arrhenius** studied acids and bases in the **1880s**. (You had to make your own entertainment in those days).

   a) Complete the sentences below which outline his theory.

      i) When mixed with ...., all acids release .... ions.

      ii) When mixed with ...., all alkalis release .... ions.

   b) It was known at the time that ammonia gas behaves as a **base**.
Explain why this prevented Arrhenius' ideas from being accepted at first.

      ....

   c) Give one other reason why Arrhenius' theory was not immediately accepted.

      ....

Q3 One definition states that acid/base reactions involve **proton transfer**. This idea allows the reaction between **hydrogen chloride gas** and **ammonia gas** to be classified as an acid/base reaction.

$$NH_3(g) + HCl(g) \rightarrow NH_4^+Cl^-(s)$$

   a) Write down the chemical symbol for a **proton**. ....

   b) Who came up with this definition of acids and bases? ....

   c) Complete the sentences to explain how the above reaction fits in with this definition.

When the two gases react, the hydrogen chloride behaves as .... by .... At the same time the ammonia behaves as .... by ....

Q4 Explain how the following **bases** produce **alkaline** solutions.

   a) potassium hydroxide, KOH ....

      ....

   b) ammonia, NH_3 ....

      ....

Chemistry 3(i) — Elements, Acids and Water

Acids, Alkalis and Titration

Q1 Say whether the statements below are **true** or **false**.

a) Ammonia is a weak acid. ....

b) Weak acids have a lower concentration of H⁺ ions in water than strong acids. ....

c) Sodium hydroxide is a weak alkali. ....

d) Strong alkalis ionise almost completely in water. ....

e) Nitric acid ionises only very slightly in water. ....

Q2 Circle the answer which best completes each of these sentences.

a) During acid/alkali titrations...

...methyl orange is always a suitable indicator.　　...the alkali must always go in the burette.

...the tap is opened fully near the end of the titration.　　...the flask is swirled regularly.

b) Phenolphthalein was added to sodium hydroxide in a flask as part of a titration with an acid. The indicator colour change was...

...yellow/orange to red.　　...red to yellow/orange.

...colourless to pink.　　...pink to colourless.

Q3 A spatula measure of a **substance X** was dissolved in some pure water and its pH measured. A value of **4.6** was obtained. A further spatula measure of X was dissolved and the pH fell to **4.2**.

a) What **instrument** can be used to measure pH accurately? ....

b) Solid X is **a weak acid / a strong acid / a weak alkali / a strong alkali**. (Circle your answer.)

c) Describe how the **concentration of H⁺ ions** changed.

....

Q4 A **titration** procedure was used to compare the **acid concentration** of some fizzy drinks. The acids present included carbonic, citric and ethanoic acid.

a) Name the independent variable and the dependent variable in this experiment.

Independent variable: ....

Dependent variable: ....

b) Suggest a suitable indicator and describe the colour change which would occur.

....

The titration values (titres) are shown in the table below.

fizzy drink	1st titre (cm³)	2nd titre (cm³)
Fizzade	15.2	14.6
Kolafizz	20.5	19.8
Cherriade	12.6	12.1

c) Which drink contained the most acid?

....

Chemistry 3(i) — Elements, Acids and Water

Titration Calculations

Q1 Work out the number of **moles** in the following solutions.

Remember, no. of moles = conc. × vol.

a) 1 dm³ of 2 mol/dm³ HCl.

....

b) 100 cm³ of 1 mol/dm³ NaOH.

....

c) 25 cm³ of 0.1 mol/dm³ HNO_3.

....

d) 10 cm³ of 0.2 mol/dm³ $Ca(OH)_2$.

....

Q2 Complete and balance the **symbol equations** for the following acid/alkali reactions.

Hint: acid + alkali → salt + water.

a) HCl + NaOH → .... + ...

b) H_2SO_4 + $Ca(OH)_2$ → .... + ...

c) H_2SO_4 + ... KOH → .... + ...

d) .... HNO_3 + $Ca(OH)_2$ → .... + ...

Q3 Work out the **masses** and **concentrations** below.

a) Work out the **mass** of acid or alkali present in each solution below.

You can look up the relative atomic masses in a periodic table — you don't have to learn them.

i) 0.5 moles of NaOH.

....

ii) 0.2 moles of H_2SO_4.

....

iii) 0.02 moles of $Ca(OH)_2$.

....

b) Work out the concentration in **g/dm³** of the solutions below.

i) 0.1 mol/dm³ potassium hydroxide (KOH) solution.

....

ii) 2 mol/dm³ nitric acid (HNO_3).

....

Chemistry 3(i) — Elements, Acids and Water

Titration Calculations

Q4 The concentration of some limewater, **Ca(OH)$_2$**, was determined by titration with hydrochloric acid, **HCl**. **50 cm^3** of limewater required **20 cm^3** of **0.1 mol/dm^3** hydrochloric acid to neutralise it. Work out the concentration of the limewater in **g/dm^3** using the steps outlined below.

a) How many moles of HCl are present in 20 cm^3 of 0.1 mol/dm^3 solution?

....

b) Complete the equation for this reaction.

.... + ... → CaCl$_2$ + ...

c) From the equation, ... mole(s) of HCl reacts with .... mole(s) of Ca(OH)$_2$.

d) Use your answer to c) to work out how many moles of Ca(OH)$_2$ there are in 50 cm^3 of limewater.

....

e) What is the concentration of the limewater in moles per dm^3?

....

f) What is the concentration of the limewater in grams per dm^3?

....

Q5 In a titration, **10 cm^3** of **sulfuric acid solution** was used to neutralise **30 cm^3** of **0.1 mol/dm^3 potassium hydroxide solution**.

$$H_2SO_4 + 2KOH \rightarrow K_2SO_4 + 2H_2O$$

a) What was the concentration of the sulfuric acid in moles per dm^3?

....

....

....

....

....

b) What is the concentration of the sulfuric acid in grams per dm^3?

....

....

Top Tips: Aargh, calculations. As if Chemistry wasn't tricky enough without maths getting involved too (but at least it's not as bad as Physics). Actually, these aren't the worst calculations as long as you tackle them in stages and know your equations.

Chemistry 3(i) — Elements, Acids and Water

Water

Q1 The diagram below shows the **water cycle**.

a) Write the correct letter (A, B, C or D) next to each label below to show where it belongs on the diagram.

air rises, water condenses ....

water flows ....

evaporation ....

rain ....

b) At which stage on the diagram is water separated from minerals in the sea? ....

c) At which stage do small amounts of minerals dissolve in water? ....

Q2 Water is sometimes known as the **universal solvent** because so many substances dissolve in it.

a) Tick the appropriate columns to show whether the compounds shown are **soluble** or **insoluble** in water.

SALT	SOLUBLE	INSOLUBLE
sodium sulfate		
ammonium chloride		
lead nitrate		
silver chloride		
lead sulfate		
potassium chloride		
barium sulfate		

b) Would you expect the following compounds to be **soluble** or **insoluble** in water? Justify your answers.

i) Potassium chromate. .... because ....

....

ii) Vanadium nitrate. .... because ....

....

Q3 Choose from the words in the box to fill in the blanks in the passage below.

power stations	alkali	fertilisers	sulfur	carbon	households
rocks	distilled	acid	car washes	pure	impure

Rainwater is usually quite .... However, it may dissolve ....

dioxide, which has been released from .... or car exhausts. This creates

harmful .... rain. As rainwater flows over fields of crops it can dissolve

chemicals from .... Minerals can also be dissolved as water passes over

.... Water has to be treated before it can be supplied to ....

Chemistry 3(i) — Elements, Acids and Water

Water

Q4 Tick the boxes next to any of these statements that are **true**.

☐ All chloride salts are soluble in water.

☐ Water is essential for life because many biological reactions take place in solution.

☐ All nitrates are soluble in water, except for silver nitrate and lead nitrate.

☐ Fertilisers are often ammonium salts which are soluble in water.

☐ Many covalent compounds like wax and petrol don't dissolve in water.

Q5 When **sodium chloride** dissolves in water, the sodium and chloride ions, **Na⁺** and **Cl⁻**, are separated by the water molecules.

a) Water can dissolve ionic compounds because of the slight charges on either side of the water molecule. In the diagram below, label the atoms in the water molecule with their chemical symbols and show where the slight negative charge and slight positive charges are found.

b) The diagram below is intended to show how water molecules interact with sodium and chloride ions when they are dissolved.

part of an NaCl crystal   dissolved sodium and chloride ions

i) Label the remaining ions in the crystal.

ii) What holds the ions in the crystal together?

....

iii) Draw **four** water molecules around **each** dissolved ion above.

Top Tips: Go back to the basics when thinking about how ions interact. Opposite charges attract (no matter how small), so a positive ion attracts a negative ion and vice versa.

Chemistry 3(i) — Elements, Acids and Water

Solubility

Q1 Match the **solubility terms** below with the descriptions given.

solvent — A solution in which no more solute will dissolve.

solute — A liquid which dissolves a solute.

solution — A substance which dissolves in a liquid.

saturated — The mixture formed when a solute dissolves in a solvent.

Q2 Look at the questions below and circle the best answer in each case.

a) The solubility of a solute is usually expressed in:

grams per 1000 grams of solvent

kilograms per 100 grams of solvent

moles per 100 grams of solvent

grams per 100 grams of solvent

b) A solution is saturated if:

the solution is colourless

some solute remains undissolved

only stirring it causes more solute to dissolve

the solution is clear

c) Gases dissolve more readily at **high** / **low** temperatures and at **high** / **low** pressures.

Q3 Choose from the words in the box to complete the passage below.

| oxygen | fertiliser | aquatic | carbon dioxide | fizzy | bleach |
| underground | pressure | nitrogen | alcoholic | chlorine | |

Gas solubility is important for .... life. Fish need dissolved .... to survive. Small amounts of .... also dissolve in water, creating a solution which is used as a .... in the textile industry and to sterilise water supplies. .... dissolves well under .... and is used to make .... drinks.

Chemistry 3(i) — Elements, Acids and Water

Solubility

Q4 Ami investigated the **solubility** of potassium chloride at different **temperatures**. She added different masses of potassium chloride to **50 g** of water and heated the solution (when necessary), stirring it continuously, until the potassium chloride just dissolved. This temperature was recorded.

mass of KCl used (g)	solubility (g / 100 g)	temperature (°C)
17	34	6
18	36	14
20		29
21		51
23		52

a) Add the missing solubility values to the tables.

b) Plot the solubility values against temperature on the grid below.

c) i) Circle the value on the grid which might be anomalous.

ii) What could Ami do to confirm that this result was anomalous?

....

....

....

d) Draw a straight line of best fit, ignoring the anomalous result.

e) Estimate the solubility of potassium chloride at:

Remember to give the correct units.

i) 20 °C .... ii) 40 °C ....

Q5 The graph shows the solubility of **potassium nitrate** and **lead nitrate** at different **temperatures**.

a) What is the solubility of potassium nitrate at **35 °C**? .... g / 100 g

b) Estimate the solubility of lead nitrate at **70 °C** by extending the line.

.... g / 100 g

c) Which of the two compounds has the greater solubility:

i) at 10 °C? .... ii) at 60 °C? ....

d) Estimate the mass of **potassium nitrate** which would **crystallise out** when a saturated solution containing 100 g of water is cooled from 50 °C to 25 °C.

....

Chemistry 3(i) — Elements, Acids and Water

Hard Water

Q1 State whether the sentences below about **hard water** are true or false.

a) Water which passes over limestone and chalk rocks becomes hard. ....

b) Water can be softened by removing chloride and carbonate ions from the water. ....

c) Adding sodium chloride is one way of removing hardness from water. ....

d) Scale is formed when soap is used with hard water. ....

e) You can remove the hardness from water by adding sodium carbonate. ....

Q2 In an experiment to investigate the **causes** of **hardness** in water, soap solution was added to different solutions. 'Five-drop portions' were added until a sustainable lather was formed.

Solution	Drops of soap solution needed to produce a lather	Observations	Drops of detergent solution needed to produce a lather
distilled water	5	no scum	5
magnesium sulfate solution	35	scum formed	5
calcium chloride solution	30	scum formed	5
sodium chloride solution	5	no scum	5

a) Why must all the solutions be prepared from distilled water rather than tap water?

....

b) i) Which compounds caused hardness in the water?

....

ii) Explain how you know. ....

....

c) What role did the test using distilled water play in the experiment?

....

d) What is the advantage of using detergent solution rather than soap for washing?

....

Q3 Hard water can cause the build-up of **scale** in pipes, boilers and kettles.

a) Why can this be a problem with kettles? ....

b) Give two **benefits** of hard water.

1. ....

2. ....

Chemistry 3(i) — Elements, Acids and Water

Hard Water

Q4 Explain how hard water becomes soft when it is passed through an **ion exchange resin**. Write an equation which includes **Na₂Resin(s)** as one of the reactants to help you.

Na₂Resin(s) + ... → .... + ...

....

....

Q5 A teacher wanted to demonstrate how chalk (composed of CaCO₃) dissolves in rainwater to produce **hard water**, and how it forms **scale** when it is boiled. She carried out the following experiments.

a) A spatula measure of powdered calcium carbonate was added to some distilled water and stirred. Why didn't the water become hard?

....

b) Carbon dioxide was bubbled through the mixture of calcium carbonate and distilled water.

i) Complete the equation below to show the reaction that took place.

CO₂(g) + H₂O(l) + CaCO₃(s) → ....(aq)

ii) Why did the water become hard?

....

c) A solution of calcium hydrogencarbonate was boiled in a beaker. As it boiled, a white precipitate formed.

Ca(HCO₃)₂(aq) → CaCO₃(s) + H₂O(l) + CO₂(g)

i) Name the white precipitate formed. ....

ii) Describe the problems that this reaction can cause when it happens in **hot water pipes**.

....

....

d) Suggest one way that the white precipitate could be removed.

....

Top Tip   Hard water isn't very exciting, but at least it's not, well, hard. The only bits that will take some learning are the equations, especially that rather nasty calcium hydrogencarbonate one.

Chemistry 3(i) — Elements, Acids and Water

Water Quality

Q1 Choose the correct option from those given. Underline your answer.

a) Which type of water is most pure?

tap water   **river water**   **distilled water**   **sea water**

b) Tap water can be passed through carbon filters. This removes:

ions which cause hardness   **chlorine taste**   **microorganisms**   **excess acidity**

Q2 Draw lines to match the **water treatment processes** to the **substances removed**.

Water Treatment Process	Substance(s) removed
filtration	harmful microorganisms
chlorination	phosphates
adding iron compounds	acidity
adding lime (calcium hydroxide)	solids

Q3 The processes A to D are used in **water purification**.

A — filtration   **B — distillation**   **C — ion exchange**   **D — boiling**

Which of these processes:

a) involves boiling and condensation? ....

b) is used to kill microorganisms? ....

c) can be carried out using a gravel bed? ....

d) is used to soften water? ....

Q4 In 1995 it was estimated that **1 billion** people did **not** have access to clean drinking water.

a) Explain why so many people in developing countries don't have access to clean water.

....

....

b) Historically, how has life expectancy been linked to the ability to supply clean water?

....

Q5 One part of water treatment involves reducing **phosphate** and **nitrate** levels in drinking water.

a) Why are these substances removed? ....

b) What can be used to reduce nitrate levels in water? ....

c) **Phosphate** levels can be reduced by adding **iron compounds**. The phosphate is precipitated out as **iron phosphate**. How is the iron phosphate removed from the water?

....

Chemistry 3(i) — Elements, Acids and Water

Mixed Questions — Chemistry 3(i)

Q1 Answer the following questions about the **periodic table**.

a) By what property did Mendeleev arrange the elements in the periodic table?
....

b) What did he do that Newlands didn't? ....

c) If an element is in Group I, how many electrons will it have in its outer electron shell? ....

d) An ion of an element has a 2+ charge. Which group is the element **most likely** to be in? ....

e) If an ion has a 1- charge, then which group is it **most likely** to be in? ....

f) Complete this table by filling in the **electronic configurations** of the elements:

You can use the periodic table to help you if you need to.

Period	Group I	Group II	Group III	Group VII	Group O
2	Li 2,1	Be	B	F	Ne
3	Na	Mg	Al	Cl	Ar 2,8,8

Q2 Many different substances can dissolve in **water**.

a) Underline any of the substances below that you would expect to be soluble in water.

ammonium nitrate   **barium sulfate**   **carbon dioxide**   **magnesium sulfate**   **lead chloride**

b) Which of the substances listed in part a) could be responsible for causing **hard water**?
....

c) Give a definition of the '**solubility**' of a substance at a particular temperature.
....
....

d) Use this solubility curve for **ammonium nitrate** to answer the following questions.

i) How much ammonium nitrate can be dissolved in 100 cm³ of water at 50 °C?
....

ii) Estimate the mass of ammonium nitrate which would crystallise out when a saturated solution containing 100 cm³ water is cooled from 50 °C to 20 °C.
....
....

e) Ammonium nitrate is a poisonous salt which would be removed from water at a water treatment works. How are nitrates removed from water?
....

Chemistry 3(i) — Elements, Acids and Water

Mixed Questions — Chemistry 3(i)

Q3 **Aqueous chlorine**, Cl₂, was added to **potassium bromide solution**, KBr. Aqueous chlorine is pale green and potassium bromide is colourless.

a) Aqueous chlorine is chlorine gas dissolved in water. Would the amount of gas that could be dissolved **increase** or **decrease** if the temperature of the solution was raised? ....

b) Complete and **balance** the following chemical equation:

.... Cl₂ (aq) + ... KBr (aq) → .... (......) + ... (......)

c) What would you observe when the two reactants are mixed?

....

d) Suggest why bromine solution will **not** react with aqueous potassium chloride.

....

Q4 Acids and bases **neutralise** one another when they are mixed together.

a) Complete the sentences below to give definitions of an **acid** and a **base**.

Acids .... H⁺ ions — they are proton ....

Bases .... H⁺ ions — they are proton ....

b) HCl is a **strong** acid. What does this mean?

....

c) Which of the acids in each of these pairs is stronger?

  i) 1 mol/dm³ HCl (pH 0) and 1 mol/dm³ HNO₃ (pH 1) ....

  ii) 1 mol/dm³ CH₃COOH (pH 2.38) and 1 mol/dm³ HCOOH (pH 1.87) ....

Q5 During a titration, 20 cm³ of 0.5 M sodium hydroxide solution was used to neutralise 25 cm³ of hydrochloric acid.

a) In a titration experiment, suggest an **indicator** to use with HCl. ....

b) What is the **concentration** of the acid, in:

  i) moles per dm³? ....

  ....

  ....

  ....

  ii) grams per dm³? ....

  ....

  ....

Chemistry 3(i) — Elements, Acids and Water

Mixed Questions — Chemistry 3(i)

Q6 The table below contains data for three elements, D, E and F, one of which is a **transition metal**.

Element	Melting point (°C)	Electrical conductivity	Density (g/cm³)
D	98	good	0.97
E	115	poor	2.07
F	1540	good	7.9

a) Which of the elements is likely to be a transition metal? Give two reasons to justify your answer.

....

....

b) Iron is a typical transition metal.

i) Why is iron used in the Haber process for the production of ammonia?

....

ii) Suggest one reason why iron, in the form of steel, is used as a structural material.

....

Q7 The elements of Group I, the alkali metals, are reactive metals.

a) Choose an **element** from the list to answer each of these questions. Use the periodic table to help you. Give:

i) the element with the lowest density. ....

ii) the element with the lowest melting point. ....

iii) the least reactive element. ....

iv) the element with the largest diameter atoms. ....

A Rubidium
B Sodium
C Potassium
D Lithium
E Francium
F Caesium

b) Complete the following sentence by circling the correct words.

> Alkali metals always form **covalent** / **ionic** compounds. They react with
> **water** / **air** to produce **hydrogen** / **oxygen** gas and a **hydroxide** / **chloride** solution.
> **Hydrogen** / **Oxygen** gas can be tested for using **a lighted splint** / **limewater**.

c) How does the reactivity of the alkali metals change as you move down the group? Explain this trend in terms of electron arrangement.

....

....

....

Chemistry 3(i) — Elements, Acids and Water

Chemistry 3(ii) — Energy and Chemical Tests

Energy

Q1 Use the words below to **complete** the blanks in the passage.

> endothermic   exothermic   energy   heat   an increase   a decrease

All chemical reactions involve changes in .... In ....
reactions, ... energy is given out to the surroundings. A thermometer will show
.... in temperature.
In .... reactions, ... energy is taken in from the
surroundings. A thermometer will show .... in temperature.

Q2 Fiz investigated the **temperature change** during a reaction. She added 25 cm³ of sodium hydroxide solution to 25 cm³ of hydrochloric acid. She used a **data logger** to measure the temperature of the reaction over the first **five** seconds.

Fiz plotted her results on the graph shown.

a) What was the increase in temperature due to the reaction?
....

b) Circle any of the words below that correctly describe the reaction in this experiment.

  neutralisation   combustion
  endothermic   respiration   exothermic

c) Why is it difficult to get **an accurate result** for the temperature change in an experiment like this?
....

Q3 **Circle** the correct words to complete each of the sentences below.

a) An example of an endothermic reaction is **photosynthesis / combustion**.

b) An example of an exothermic reaction is **photosynthesis / neutralisation**.

c) Bond breaking is an **exothermic / endothermic** process.

d) Bond forming is an **exothermic / endothermic** process.

Q4 During the following reaction the reaction mixture's temperature **increases**.

$$AB + C \longrightarrow AC + B$$

a) Is the reaction exothermic or endothermic? ....

b) Which bond is stronger, A–B or A–C? Explain your answer.
....

Energy and Fuels

Q1 Answer the following questions on **fuels** and **calorimetry**.

a) Burning fuel releases energy. Is it an endothermic or exothermic reaction? ....

b) Why is **copper** used as the material for calorimetry cans?
....

c) Why is the experimental energy content of a fuel often much less than the actual energy content?
....

Q2 In a calorimetry experiment, **0.7 g** of petrol raised the temperature of **50 g** of water by **30.5 °C**.

a) Given that it takes **4.2 J** to raise the temperature of **1 g** of water by **1 °C**, calculate the energy gained by the water.

Use: energy gained = 4.2 × mass of water × temperature rise

....

b) Use your answer to **a)** to calculate the energy produced per gram of petrol. Give your answer in units of **kJ/g**.

Use: energy per gram = energy produced ÷ mass of fuel used

....

Q3 A petrol alternative, **fuel X**, has been sent for testing. A scientist tests it using calorimetry. Burning **0.8 g** of fuel X raises the temperature of **50 g** of water by **27 °C**.

a) Calculate the energy produced per gram of fuel X.

....
....

b) Look at your answers to **a)** and **Q2 b)**. Using this evidence only, decide whether petrol or fuel X would make the better fuel. Explain your choice.

....

Q4 Burning fuels has both **social** and **environmental** consequences.

a) Name the greenhouse gas released when fossil fuels are burnt. ....

b) Give a possible consequence of increasing levels of greenhouse gases in the atmosphere.

....

c) Renewable energy sources have been proposed as a solution to the problems caused by burning fossil fuels. Give three examples of renewable energy sources.

....

d) Explain one potential **economic problem** caused by our reliance on crude oil.

....
....

Chemistry 3(ii) — Energy and Chemical Tests

Bond Energies

Q1 The **energy level diagrams** below represent the energy changes in five chemical reactions.

A **B** **C** **D** **E**

Which diagram(s) show:

a) an exothermic reaction? .... b) the reaction with the largest activation energy? ....

c) an endothermic reaction? .... d) a catalysed form of the reaction shown in A? ....

Q2 Answer the following questions about **energy changes**.

a) What does the symbol ΔH represent? ....

b) A chemical reaction has a ΔH of +42 kJ/mol. Is this reaction exothermic or endothermic?

....

c) Is **bond forming** an exothermic or an endothermic process? ....

d) What is the **activation energy** of a reaction?

....

e) What effect do catalysts have on chemical reactions, and why?

....

....

Q3 Here is an energy level diagram for a reaction.

a) What is the value of ΔH for the reaction?

....

b) What is the activation energy?

Remember to show whether your value is +ve or –ve.

....

c) This reaction is reversible.
What is the activation energy of the reverse reaction?

....

Top Tips: It's easy to mix up the two types of reaction. So just learn this: exothermic = energy given out = negative ΔH = energy of products lower than energy of reactants = more energy released in making new bonds than needed for breaking old bonds. That's all there is to it. Hmm.

Chemistry 3(ii) — Energy and Chemical Tests

Bond Energies

Q4 The equations below show the combustion of **methane**.

$$CH_4 + 2O_2 \rightarrow CO_2 + 2H_2O$$

H–C–H (with H above and H below) + 2 O=O ⟹ O=C=O + 2 H–O–H

Use the bond energies given below to answer the questions.

C–H = +412 kJ/mol   O=O = +498 kJ/mol   C=O = +743 kJ/mol   O–H = +463 kJ/mol

a) What is the total energy required to break all the bonds in the reactants?

....

Carefully count how many of each type of bond there are.

b) What is the total energy released when the bonds in the products are formed?

....

c) Use your answers to a) and b) to calculate ΔH for the reaction.

Don't forget to include a '+' or a '–'.

....

Q5 Calculate ΔH for the combustion of hydrazine, N_2H_4.

$$N_2H_4 + O_2 \rightarrow N_2 + 2H_2O$$

H₂N–NH₂ + O=O ⟹ N≡N + 2 H–O–H

N–N = +158 kJ/mol
N≡N = +945 kJ/mol
N–H = +391 kJ/mol

Use the bond energies above and those given in Q4.

....

....

Q6 Calculate ΔH for the combustion of ethane.

$$2C_2H_6 + 7O_2 \rightarrow 4CO_2 + 6H_2O$$

2 H–C–C–H (with H's) + 7 O=O ⟹ 4 O=C=O + 6 H–O–H

a) Use the bond energies given in Q4, and **C–C = +348 kJ/mol**.

....

....

b) Use your answer to b) to calculate the energy change when 1 mole of ethane is burned.

....

Energy and Food

Q1 Circle the correct word from each pair to complete the passage below.

Foods are a store of **heat** / **chemical** energy. This energy is released in our bodies by **respiration** / **movement**. Foods containing a high proportion of **carbohydrate** / **fat** release the most energy.

Q2 a) If the food you eat contains **more energy** than your body needs, what happens to the **extra** energy?

....

b) What is a calorie-controlled diet?

....

Q3 Vera studies the **nutritional information** on a box of bran flakes and on an egg carton.

EGGS (per 100 g)	
Energy	147 kcal
Protein	12.5 g
Carbohydrate	trace
Fat	10.8 g
Sodium	0.1 g

Bran flakes (per 100 g)	
Energy	331 kcal
Protein	11.1 g
Carbohydrate	64.6 g
Fat	3.2 g
Sodium	0.6 g

a) Which food provides more fat per 100 g?

....

b) Vera eats a serving of 30 g of bran flakes. How much energy does this provide?

....

Q4 Food energy is often measured in **calories**.

a) Complete the following:

1 calorie is the amount of energy needed to raise the temperature of ....

by .... **There are** .... **J in 1 calorie.**

b) What is the difference between a calorie and a Calorie?

....

c) A chocolate bar contains 270 kcal of energy. What is this value in kJ?

....

Q5 Complete the word equation for **respiration** below.

glucose + ... → .... + ... + ENERGY

Chemistry 3(ii) — Energy and Chemical Tests

Tests for Cations

Q1 What are **cations**? Explain why the prefix '**cat**' is used.

....

....

Think about the electrodes used in electrolysis.

Q2 Les had five samples of **metal compounds**. He tested each one by placing a small amount on the end of a wire and putting it into a Bunsen flame. He observed the **colour of flame** produced.

a) Draw lines to match each of Les's observations to the metal cation producing the coloured flame.

brick-red flame		Na^+
yellow-orange flame		Ba^{2+}
crimson flame		K^+
green flame		Ca^{2+}
lilac flame		Li^+

b) Les wants to recommend a compound to use in a firework at a fundraising event for his local football team. Which of the following compounds should he recommend in order for the firework to explode in his team's colour, lilac? Circle your answer.

silver nitrate   sodium chloride   barium sulfate   potassium nitrate   calcium carbonate

Q3 Cilla adds a few drops of **NaOH** solution to solutions of different **metal compounds**.

a) Complete her table of results.

Metal Cation	Colour of Precipitate
Fe^{2+}	
	blue
Fe^{3+}	
Al^{3+}	

b) Complete the balanced ionic equation for the reaction of iron(II) ions with hydroxide ions.

Fe^{2+}(........) + ... OH^-(aq) → .... (s)

c) Write a balanced ionic equation for the reaction of **iron(III) ions** with hydroxide ions. Include state symbols.

....

d) Cilla adds a few drops of sodium hydroxide solution to **aluminium sulfate solution**. She continues adding sodium hydroxide to excess. What would she observe at each stage?

....

Tests for Cations

Q4 The **ammonium ion** can also be tested for be adding sodium hydroxide.

a) What is the chemical formula of the ammonium ion? ....

b) What pungent gas is released if sodium hydroxide is added to a solution of ammonium ions? Give its name and its formula.

Name: .... Formula: ....

c) What test could you use to identify this gas (other than relying on your sense of smell)?
....

d) When ammonium ions react with hydroxide ions only two products are formed. Use this information to write a balanced ionic equation for the reaction. Include state symbols.
....

Q5 Select compounds from the box to match the following statements.

KCl	LiCl	FeSO$_4$	NH$_4$Cl	FeCl$_3$	Al$_2$(SO$_4$)$_3$
NaCl	CuSO$_4$	CaCl$_2$	MgCl$_2$		BaCl$_2$

a) This compound forms a blue precipitate with sodium hydroxide solution. ....

b) This compound gives a crimson flame in a flame test. ....

c) This compound forms a white precipitate with sodium hydroxide that dissolves if excess sodium hydroxide is added. ....

d) This compound forms a green precipitate with sodium hydroxide solution. ....

e) This compound forms a reddish brown precipitate with sodium hydroxide solution. ....

f) This compound reacts with sodium hydroxide to release a pungent gas. ....

g) This compound reacts with sodium hydroxide to form a white precipitate, and it also gives a brick-red flame in a flame test. ....

Top Tips: Right, this stuff needs to be learnt, and learnt properly. Otherwise you'll be stuck in your exam staring at a question about what colour some random solution goes when you add something you've never heard of to it, and all you'll know is that ammonia smells of cat wee. That's not going to impress anyone.

Chemistry 3(ii) — Energy and Chemical Tests

Tests for Anions

Q1 Give the chemical formulas (including charge) of the **anions** present in the following compounds.

a) barium sulfate ....   b) potassium iodide ....

c) magnesium carbonate ....   d) ammonium nitrate ....

Q2 Use the words given to complete the passage below.

carbon dioxide   limewater   colour   acid   white   black
A test for the presence of carbonates in an unidentified substance involves reacting it with dilute .... If carbonates are present then .... will be formed. You can test for this by bubbling it through .... to see if it becomes milky. Some carbonates also undergo distinctive .... changes on heating. Copper carbonate changes from green to .... and zinc carbonate changes from .... to yellow on heating.

Q3 Answer the following questions on testing for **sulfate** and **nitrate** ions.

a) Which two reactants are used to test for sulfate ions?

....

b) What would you see after adding these reactants to a sulfate compound?

....

c) Which two reactants are used to test for nitrate ions?

....

Q4 Deirdre wants to find out if a soluble compound contains **chloride**, **bromide** or **iodide** ions. Explain how she could do this.

....

....

....

Q5 Complete the following symbol equations for reactions involved in **anion** tests.

a) $Ag^+(aq)$ + ... → $AgCl(s)$

b) $2HCl(aq) + Na_2CO_3(s)$ → $2NaCl(aq)$ + ...(l) + ...(g)

c) .... + ... → $BaSO_4(s)$

d) $CuCO_3(s)$ → ....(s) + ...(g)

Chemistry 3(ii) — Energy and Chemical Tests

Tests for Organic Compounds

Q1 Answer the following questions on heating **organic compounds**.

a) What colour is the flame when organic compounds are burnt in air?

....

b) Gus ignites two samples of hydrocarbons. One is propane, C_3H_8, and the other is octane, C_8H_{18}. Which sample will burn with a smokier flame? Explain why.

....

Q2 Pauline investigates the properties of two liquid organic compounds. She adds 1 cm³ of **bromine water** to a 5 cm³ sample of each compound. She then shakes each sample for 10 seconds and records her observations.

a) i) Give three examples of controlled variables in Pauline's investigation.

....

ii) Explain why she controlled these variables.

....

Pauline presents her results in the table shown.

Organic compound	Colour of bromine water after shaking
A	colourless
B	orange

b) Which compound is a **saturated** hydrocarbon? ....

c) Which compound could be an **alkene**? ....

d) Which of the following could be the structural formula of organic compound A? Circle all possibilities.

Q3 **Hydrocarbons** are compounds that contain **hydrogen** and **carbon only**.

a) What two products are formed by the **complete combustion** of hydrocarbons?

....

b) Complete the word and symbol equations for the complete combustion of ethene, C_2H_4. Balance the symbol equation.

ethene + ... → .... + ...

C_2H_4 + ... O_2 → .... + ...

c) What other products might form if the air supply for the combustion were reduced?

....

Chemistry 3(ii) — Energy and Chemical Tests

Tests for Organic Compounds

Q4 A sample of a hydrocarbon is burnt completely in air. **8.8 g** of **carbon dioxide** and **5.4 g** of **water** are produced.

Multiply the mass of CO_2 produced by the proportion of carbon in CO_2.

a) Calculate the mass of **carbon** in the carbon dioxide.

....

....

b) Calculate the mass of **hydrogen** in the water.

....

....

c) Calculate the number of **moles** of carbon and of hydrogen in the sample of this hydrocarbon.

No. of moles = mass ÷ relative atomic mass.

....

....

Find the simplest ratio of moles of C : moles of H.

d) What is the **empirical formula** of this hydrocarbon?

....

....

Q5 a) A sample of a hydrocarbon is burnt completely in air. **4.4 g** of carbon dioxide and **1.8 g** of water are formed. What is the **empirical formula** of the hydrocarbon?

....

....

....

....

b) An organic compound contains only carbon, hydrogen and oxygen. **0.8 g** of the compound is burnt completely in air. **1.1 g** of carbon dioxide and **0.9 g** of water are formed. What is the compound's **empirical formula**?

Watch out — some of the oxygen in the products came from the air, NOT the organic compound. You need to subtract the masses of C and H from the compound's mass to find the mass of O.

....

....

....

....

Chemistry 3(ii) — Energy and Chemical Tests

Instrumental Methods

Q1 Forensic scientists use **instrumental methods** to analyse substances found at crime scenes.

a) Suspects in criminal cases can only be held for a short period of time without being charged. In light of this, why are instrumental methods useful for preparing forensic evidence?

....

b) Give **two** other advantages of using instrumental methods.

....

Q2 **Atomic absorption spectroscopy** is used to identify elements. Ian compares the **absorption spectrum** of an unknown element to a set of absorption spectra from known elements.

unknown element   cadmium, Cd   lithium, Li   sodium, Na

a) Identify the **unknown** element. ....

b) Give **one** industry where this method is used. ....

Q3 Answer the following questions on mass spectrometry.

a) A sample of a steel is vaporised and a mass spectrum taken. The spectrum identifies elements with relative atomic masses of 52, 55 and 56. What **elements** are present in the steel?

....

b) A mass spectrum shows that an alkene has a relative molecular mass of 70. What is the molecular formula of the alkene?

Alkenes have the general formula C_nH_{2n}.

....

c) A mass spectrum of a **pure** sample of the element antimony is taken. However two relative atomic masses are detected by the spectrometer, one at 121 and one at 123. Suggest why **two** relative atomic masses were detected.

....

Q4 **NMR spectroscopy** is a powerful instrumental method of analysis.

a) What do the letters **NMR** stand for? ....

b) What type of compound can this method analyse? ....

c) Which **atoms** in these compounds does NMR give you information about?

....

Chemistry 3(ii) — Energy and Chemical Tests

Identifying Unknown Substances

Q1 Over 2000 years ago Archimedes developed a **test** for **gold**. He compared the density of a crown supposedly made from gold with the density of a sample of pure gold.

Name two modern instrumental methods that could be used to test whether a sample is gold.

....

Q2 Mo wants to identify an unknown **crystalline solid** (compound Z). She carries out a series of tests on separate samples of the solid, and records her observations in the following table.

TEST	OBSERVATION
Place a small sample of the solid in a Bunsen flame.	Flame becomes a lilac colour.
Add 5 cm³ of hydrochloric acid.	No change.
Dissolve in water. Add a few drops of NaOH solution.	No change.
Dissolve in water. Add 2 cm³ of dilute nitric acid followed by 2 cm³ of silver nitrate solution.	A yellow precipitate is formed.

a) Which cation is present in compound Z? Explain how you know.

....

b) Which anion is present in compound Z? Explain how you know.

....

c) Mo is provided with a different sample of crystalline solid, compound Y. She again carries out a series of tests on separate samples of the solid, and again records her observations in a table.

TEST	OBSERVATION
Place a small sample of the solid in a Bunsen flame.	No change.
Add 5 cm³ of hydrochloric acid.	No change.
Dissolve in water. Add 2 cm³ of dilute hydrochloric acid followed by 2 cm³ of barium chloride solution.	A white precipitate forms.
Dissolve in water. Add a few drops of NaOH solution and test any gas given off with damp red litmus paper.	Litmus paper turns blue.

Use this information to identify compound Y.

....

Q3 You are provided with a sample of a crystalline solid. Describe an experimental procedure you could use to confirm that the solid is **iron(III) nitrate**.

....

....

....

....

Chemistry 3(ii) — Energy and Chemical Tests

Identifying Unknown Substances

Q4 Billy wants to find out whether a sample of an organic compound is **ethane** or **ethanol**.

ethane | ethanol (structural diagrams)

He uses mass spectrometry and finds that the relative molecular mass (M_r) of the compound is 46.

a) Identify the compound.

....

....

b) Name one other instrumental method that Billy could have used for this identification.

....

Q5 An organic compound contains atoms of carbon, hydrogen and oxygen only. **1 g** of the compound burns completely in air to form **1.37 g** of carbon dioxide and **1.12 g** of water. Mass spectrometry shows that the M_r of the compound is **32**, and IR spectrometry suggests it contains an **O–H bond**.

a) Use the combustion information to calculate the **empirical formula** for the compound.

....

....

....

....

b) What is the **molecular formula** of the compound?

....

c) Use your answer to b) and the information from the IR spectrum to draw the **structural formula** of the compound in the space below. Show all the **bonds** clearly in your diagram.

Top Tips: When it comes to identifying compounds, you'll need to apply what you've learned in a few different areas. You've got to know the tests for cations and anions, and be able to work out empirical formulas with your eyes shut. And don't forget those instrumental methods of analysis either.

Chemistry 3(ii) — Energy and Chemical Tests

Mixed Questions — Chemistry 3(ii)

Q1 Aerobic respiration is the process of breaking down food using oxygen to release energy.

sugar + oxygen ⟶ carbon dioxide + water + energy

a) Is this an **exothermic** or an **endothermic** reaction? Explain your answer.

....

b) Choose the correct words to complete this statement about the above equation.

> The energy needed to **break** the bonds in the reactants is **greater than / less than** the energy released when the bonds in the products are **formed**.

c) Describe one method that could be used to find the amount of energy in a food or a fuel.

....

....

d) A 0.5 g sample of sugar is burned and releases enough energy to raise the temperature of 100 g of water by 15 °C. Calculate the energy produced per gram of sugar.

....

....

Q2 Stanley is trying to identify a mystery substance.

First he adds a few drops of sodium hydroxide solution to a solution of the mystery compound.

a) What result would you expect Stanley to see if the mystery compound contained Fe^{2+} ions?

....

b) In fact, a blue precipitate forms. What can Stanley conclude?

....

c) Write down an **ionic equation** for the formation of this blue precipitate.

....

d) Stanley suspects that his compound is a sulfate. Describe a test he could do to see if he's right.

....

....

e) Stanley does the test for a sulfate, and sees a white precipitate form in the solution.

Write down the formula of Stanley's mystery compound. ....

Chemistry 3(ii) — Energy and Chemical Tests

Mixed Questions on Chemistry 3(ii)

Q3 The average adult woman needs **2000 kcal** of energy from her food each day.

a) How much is this in kJ? ....

b) What will happen to the weight of an average adult woman who consumes 8000 kJ per day?

....

Q4 The diagram shows the progress of a reaction which was carried out twice, once with a **catalyst** and once without.

a) Label the **overall energy change** of the reaction with the symbol ΔH.

b) Which reaction used a **catalyst**, A or B? ....

c) Does the graph represent an exothermic or an endothermic reaction?

....

d) Ammonia (NH$_3$) is the only product formed in the reaction between nitrogen gas (N$_2$) and hydrogen gas (H$_2$). The reaction is catalysed by iron.

   i) Write a balanced symbol equation for this reaction. ....

   ii) Calculate the energy change for the reaction using the following bond energies.
   N≡N = +945 kJ/mol, H−H = +436 kJ/mol, N−H = +391 kJ/mol

   ....

   ....

   iii) The energy change for the reaction H$_2$(g) + I$_2$(s) → 2HI(g) is **+53 kJ/mol**.
   Do you think that the energy level diagram above might represent this reaction, or is it more likely to represent the reaction in which ammonia is formed? Explain your answer.

   ....

   ....

Q5 A chemist made an organic compound, X. On analysis a sample of the compound was found to contain **240 g** of **carbon**, **160 g** of **oxygen** and **60 g** of **hydrogen**.

a) Calculate the empirical formula of compound X.

....

....

b) When this compound was added to bromine water, the bromine water stayed brown. What does this show?

....

Chemistry 3(ii) — Energy and Chemical Tests

Mixed Questions on Chemistry 3(ii)

Q6 Mary wants to identify a sample of a **white crystalline solid**.

She dissolves the sample in distilled water and carries out some tests in separate test tubes. She records her observations in the table below.

Test tube	Test	Observation
A	Add a few drops of NaOH solution, and test any gas given off with damp red litmus paper.	Litmus paper turned blue.
B	Add some dilute HNO_3 followed by a few drops of silver nitrate solution.	White precipitate formed.

a) What gas was given off in test tube A? ....

b) Write an **ionic equation** for the reaction that took place in test tube B.

....

c) Name the original white crystalline solid. ....

Q7 Modern **instrumental methods** have made it much easier to identify unknown substances.

a) Name four instrumental techniques that can be used to identify unknown substances.

1. ....

2. ....

3. ....

4. ....

Note: some instrumental methods may be less useful than others.

b) Give three practical uses of such techniques.

....

....

c) There have been huge advances in electronics and computing over the last 10-20 years. What impact has this had on the development of instrumental methods for chemical analysis?

....

....

Q8 Which ions would give the following results?

a) Brick-red colour in a flame test. ....

b) Releases a gas that turns limewater cloudy when added to an acid. ....

c) Forms a reddish brown precipitate when NaOH solution is added. ....

d) Forms a white precipitate after dilute HCl followed by $BaCl_2$ is added. ....

Chemistry 3(ii) — Energy and Chemical Tests

Answers

Chemistry 1a — Products from Rocks

Chemistry 1a — Products from Rocks

Page 1 — Atoms and Elements

Q1 a) [diagram labelled: neutron, proton, electron]
b) Diagram should be correctly labelled as above
Q2 copper and oxygen should be circled
Q3 All the atoms in gold and aluminium are the same type but in water and sugar there are atoms of more than one element.
Q4 a) protons
b) protons, neutrons
c) shells/energy levels/orbitals, nucleus
d) proton, electron

Page 2 — The Periodic Table

Q1 a) A group in the periodic table is a **vertical** line of elements.
b) Most of the elements in the periodic table are **metals**.
c) The elements between group II and group III are called **transition** metals.
d) Non-metals are on the **right-hand** side of the periodic table.
e) Elements in the same group have **similar** properties.
Q2 Any two of: neon, krypton, helium, xenon, and radon.
Q3

Element	Symbol	Reaction with magnesium	Formula of substance formed
Fluorine	F	very fast reaction	MgF_2
Chlorine	Cl	burns quickly	$MgCl_2$
Bromine	Br	moderate reaction	$MgBr_2$

Q4 Elements in the same group in the periodic table have similar properties. The periodic table helped scientists to identify the missing element because they were able to predict the properties it would have.

Pages 3-4 — Compounds and Mixtures

Q1 a) True
b) False
c) False
d) True
Q2 The missing words are: electrons, compounds, separate, different, separate, bonds.
Q3 The hydrocarbons all have different boiling points. During distillation the oil is heated and the different hydrocarbons boil off at different temperatures. The hydrocarbons can then be condensed individually and the crude oil is successfully separated.
Q4 a) elements
b) compound
c) A chemical reaction between the magnesium and the oxygen.
d) magnesium + oxygen → magnesium oxide
e) Before heating (because mixtures are much easier to separate using physical methods than compounds).
Q5 $Al(NO_3)_3$ because it contains three nitrogen atoms.

Pages 5-6 — Balancing Equations

Q1 a) Correctly balanced
b) Incorrectly balanced
c) Incorrectly balanced
d) Correctly balanced
e) Correctly balanced
Q2 The third equation should be circled.
Q3 a) The reactants are methane and oxygen, and the products are carbon dioxide and water.
b) methane + oxygen → carbon dioxide + water
c) $CH_4 + 2O_2 \rightarrow CO_2 + 2H_2O$
Q4 a) $2Na + Cl_2 \rightarrow 2NaCl$
b) $4Li + O_2 \rightarrow 2Li_2O$
c) $MgCO_3 + 2HCl \rightarrow MgCl_2 + H_2O + CO_2$
d) $2Li + 2H_2O \rightarrow 2LiOH + H_2$
Q5 a) $CuO + 2HBr \rightarrow CuBr_2 + H_2O$
b) $H_2 + Br_2 \rightarrow 2HBr$
c) $2Mg + O_2 \rightarrow 2MgO$
d) $2NaOH + H_2SO_4 \rightarrow Na_2SO_4 + 2H_2O$
Q6 a) $3NaOH + AlBr_3 \rightarrow 3NaBr + Al(OH)_3$
b) $2FeCl_2 + Cl_2 \rightarrow 2FeCl_3$
c) $N_2 + 3H_2 \rightarrow 2NH_3$
d) $4Fe + 3O_2 \rightarrow 2Fe_2O_3$
e) $4NH_3 + 5O_2 \rightarrow 4NO + 6H_2O$

Pages 7-10 — Using Limestone

Q1 a) calcium carbonate
b) calcium oxide
Q2 The missing words are: limestone, concrete, sand / sodium carbonate, sodium carbonate / sand.
Q3 a) calcium oxide (quicklime), carbon dioxide
b) magnesium oxide
c) $CuCO_3 \rightarrow CuO + CO_2$
Q4 a) calcium carbonate → calcium oxide + carbon dioxide
b) To neutralise soils that are acidic.
Q5 a) Thermal decomposition is when a substance breaks up as it is heated.
b) Calcium oxide will react with water to give an alkaline substance. You could prove this using universal indicator (it would turn blue or purple). Calcium carbonate would remain neutral.
c) Pass the gas produced through limewater. The limewater will go cloudy/milk/white, proving that carbon dioxide is present.
Q6 a) The limestone in the Peak District is very pure.
b) About 1.7 million tonnes (8.5 ÷ 5).
c) It is used in agriculture and burned in lime kilns.
d) Any three from the following: increased traffic, spoiling the look of the landscape, discouraging tourism, noise, dust, damage to habitats and the environment.
e) i) canals and railways
ii) by road / by lorry
f) Answer will depend on student's opinion, but they are likely to say that they are against it because the article focuses on the problems associated with quarrying rather than the benefits it has.
g)

Use	Percentage	Total amount quarried in tonnes
Aggregate (for road-building etc.)	55.8%	(8500000 ÷ 100) ×55.8 = 4743000
Cement	23%	(8500000 ÷ 100) ×23 = 1955000
Chemicals	17%	(8500000 ÷ 100) ×17 = 1445000
Iron and steel	4%	(8500000 ÷ 100) ×4 = 340000
Agriculture	0.2%	(8500000 ÷ 100) ×0.2 = 17000

Q7 Granite, paint and bricks should be circled.
Q8 a) neutralisation
b) The limestone removes sulfur dioxide from the smoke emitted from the power stations. This helps to reduce acid rain.

Chemistry 1a — Products from Rocks

Q9 a) Any two problems, for example: noise, dust, loss of habitats for plants and animals and increased traffic.
b) Quarries provide employment for local people which can provide a boost to the local economy. There may also be improvements to infrastructure such as roads, recreational and health facilities. After extraction has finished at a quarry the site may be turned into a wildlife habitat or recreational area.
Q10 a) Wood rots, is damaged by insects and is flammable. Concrete is not affected by any of these problems.
b) Metals corrode but concrete doesn't.
c) Bricks are made to a set size and shape but concrete can be poured into moulds of any size and shape.

Pages 11-12 — Properties of Metals

Q1 a) the transition metals
b) They are not very reactive and they conduct electricity well.
Q2 a) Metal 3 because it has the best heat conduction, and is strong and resistant to corrosion.
b) Metal 2 because it is the strongest, isn't too expensive and won't corrode too much. (Accept metal 3.)
c) Metal 1 because it is most resistant to corrosion so it will last a long time.
Q3 Desirable qualities in a metal used to make knives and forks would be: strong, resistant to corrosion, visually attractive / shiny, non-toxic.
Q4 a) A and B
b) A, because it took least time for the end that wasn't near the heat source to heat up.
Q5 a) [diagram showing free electrons and metal atoms arranged in a lattice of + ions]
b) There are a lot of free electrons in a metal because of the way they are bonded.
Q6 Any three from: good conductor of electricity, good conductor of heat, strong, easily bendable, malleable.

Pages 13-14 — Metals from Rocks

Q1 a) It is too impure to conduct electricity well.
b) Impure copper (obtained e.g. by reduction with carbon) is purified using electrolysis.
c) Water pipes (other answers possible, e.g. making coins).
Q2 Two reasons such as: There is a limited supply of copper. There is an increasing demand for copper. To reduce the amount of material going into landfill. Because it requires less energy than extracting new copper.
Q3 a) The company will be able to sell the copper they extract from other companies' waste to make money. It will also have environmental benefits.
b) Extracting copper by electrolysis uses a lot more energy than using bacteria. Using the bacteria reduces the amount of fossil fuels that are burnt, which has benefits for the environment, e.g. less acid rain.
Q4 oxygen and sulfur

Q5 Gold is less common than iron, which makes it expensive and this means that it is worth extracting it from low-grade ores. Iron is less valuable, and more common, so it is only economic to extract it from high-grade ores.
Q6 Social factors include: new jobs available for locals, improved local services, influx of people might put strain on local services.
Economic factors include: more money in local economy, more goods made from the extracted metal are available.
Environmental factors include: pollution such as dust, noise and emissions from vehicles, habitat destruction, scarring of the landscape, after extraction the area may be turned into a conservation area.

Page 15 — The Reactivity Series

Q1 a) Because zinc is more reactive than copper.
b) No, because zinc is less reactive than aluminium so it wouldn't be able to push the aluminium out and bond to the oxygen.
Q2 a) The wood.
b) Copper is very unreactive so the reaction would happen at a relatively low temperature, meaning it would be able to take place in a domestic fire.
c) A good way of supplying electricity / the electric battery (which was invented in 1800) / electrolysis.
Q3 Missing words are: carbon, below, reduction, electrolysis more.
Q4 The order of reactivity, from most to least is: dekium, candium, bodium, antium.

Pages 16-17 — Making Metals More Useful

Q1 a) A mixture of two or more metals or a mixture of a metal and a non-metal.
b) By adding small amounts of carbon or other metals to the iron.
Q2
Metal / Alloy	What has been added	Use
low-carbon steel	0.1% carbon	car bodies
iron from a blast furnace	nothing	ornamental railings
high-carbon steel	1.5% carbon	blades for tools
stainless steel	chromium	cutlery

Q3 a) copper
b) nickel
c) silver, copper or nickel
Q4 [diagram of layers of atoms] — layers of atoms can slide over each other so the iron is easy to bend and shape
Q5 a) 37.5% (9 ÷ 24 × 100 = 37.5)
b) 9-carat gold is harder than pure gold because it is an alloy and so it contains different sized atoms. The atoms in 9-carat gold can't slide over each other as easily as the ones in pure gold can.
Q6 a) Any sensible answer, e.g. in aeroplane wings, for making spectacle frames.
b) They have an ability to return to their original shape if they have been bent out of shape.
c) They are currently very expensive. They suffer more from metal fatigue than ordinary metals.

Chemistry 1a — Products from Rocks

Page 18 — More About Metals

Q1 a)

Property	Aluminium	Titanium
Density	low	low
Reactivity	**high**	**low**
Strength	**low**	**high**
Corrosion resistance	high	high
Cost	**high**	**(very) high**

b) Titanium has good corrosion resistance, a low density and is strong.

Q2 With aluminium the aluminium oxide layer on the outside of the aluminium slowly dissolves in the acid. As soon as it has dissolved the acid rapidly attacks the reactive metal. Titanium does not react with dilute hydrochloric acid at all.

Q3 Aluminium is recycled because it takes a lot of energy to extract it from its ore, so even though it is very common extracting new aluminium is very expensive. Gold is recycled because it is rare and so it's too valuable to throw away.

Page 19 — Fractional Distillation of Crude Oil

Q1 a) Crude oil is a **mixture** of different molecules.
b) The molecules in crude oil **aren't** chemically bonded to each other.
c) If crude oil were heated the **last** thing to boil off would be bitumen
d) Diesel has **larger** molecules than petrol.

Q2 (Diagram of fractional distillation column, from top to bottom: petrol, kerosene, diesel, oil, bitumen; crude oil input at bottom)

Q3 The larger the molecule the higher the boiling/condensing point.

Q4 Oil is pumped in at the bottom and the fractions are continuously removed.

Page 20 — Properties and Uses of Crude Oil

Q1 a) methane, ethane, propane, butane (structural formulae shown)
b) butane

Q2 a) The longer the alkane molecule the **more** viscous (gloopy) it is
b) The shorter the alkane molecule the **more** volatile it is.
c) A very volatile liquid is one with a **low** boiling point.

Q3 a) C_nH_{2n+2}
b) $C_{20}H_{42}$ (n = 20 so 2n + 2 = (2 × 20) + 2 = 42)

Q4 a) Oils with long carbon chains are very gloopy and so they cling to the moving parts of an engine, preventing damage.
b) Using a hydrocarbon with fewer carbon atoms would be problematic because it would vaporise when the engine got hot.

Page 21 — Using Crude Oil as a Fuel

Q1 E.g. petrol, diesel, kerosene, and gases such as propane and butane.

Q2 a) Solar power doesn't work in all places / it wouldn't be possible to use solar power at night.
b) The wind wouldn't always be blowing when someone wanted to use the oven.
c) Nuclear substances would be very dangerous if they leaked / it would be very expensive to develop a way of storing the fuel in a safe way.

Q3 a) When oil is transported by ship there is the possibility of spills into the sea. Crude oil is poisonous to birds and sea creatures.
b) Burning oil products forms substances that cause acid rain, global warming and global dimming.

Q4 New reserves of oil have been discovered since the 1960s. Also, new methods of extraction mean that oil that was once too expensive or difficult to extract can now be used.

Q5 Most technology around today is set up to use crude oil fractions as fuel and converting to alternatives would be time-consuming and costly. We need more energy than can currently be created using alternatives alone. We're simply not ready to stop using crude oil as our main source of fuel.

Page 22-24 — Environmental Problems

Q1 The main cause of acid rain is... sulfur dioxide.
Acid rain kills trees and... acidifies lakes.
Limestone buildings and statues are affected by... acid rain.
In clouds sulfur dioxide reacts with water to make... sulfuric acid.

Q2 Ways of reducing acid rain include:
Removing the sulfur from the fuel before it is burnt (using low-sulfur fuels).
Fitting cars with catalytic converters.
Using scrubbers in power station chimneys to remove sulfur dioxide from emissions.

Q3 a) Hydrocarbon + oxygen → carbon dioxide + water
b) i) $CH_4 + 2O_2 \rightarrow CO_2 + 2H_2O$
ii) $C_3H_8 + 5O_2 \rightarrow 3CO_2 + 4H_2O$

Q4 a) Carbon monoxide and carbon particles are formed when there is not enough oxygen for a hydrocarbon fuel to burn completely.
b) Carbon monoxide is dangerous because it is poisonous. (It combines with haemoglobin preventing your blood from carrying as much oxygen.)

Q5 a) The percentage of carbon dioxide in the atmosphere is increasing at an increasing (exponential) rate.
b) The burning of fossil fuels for energy.
c) The average temperature is increasing.

Q6 a) water
b) When hydrogen is used as a fuel no carbon dioxide is produced so it doesn't contribute to global warming. It doesn't produce particulates either. Also it doesn't produce sulfur dioxide so it doesn't cause acid rain.
c) Hydrogen-powered vehicles are very expensive because the engines they use are expensive. Hydrogen is difficult to store, which makes it awkward to use as a fuel. Fuelling stations would need to be adapted / converted. Hydrogen would need to be produced from non-fossil fuel sources.

Chemistry 1b — Oils, Earth and Atmosphere

Q7 a) water and carbon dioxide
b) It releases no more carbon dioxide than the sugar cane took in (by photosynthesis) when it was growing.
Q8 a) carbon dioxide and water
b) The production of biogas is slow at low temperatures.
Q9 a) i) Installing Acid Gas Scrubbers in chimneys to prevent the sulfur dioxide from being emitted.
ii) Development of more efficient engines and alternative fuels.
b) Answers may include: walking/cycling instead of using vehicles, recycling paper, metals, glass and plastics, avoiding foods that have travelled a long way / buying locally produced food, saving electricity by turning lights off, not leaving electrical devices on stand-by, not flying (using other modes of transport that use less fossil fuels), etc.
c) Answer will depend on student's opinion — may argue that everyone who lives on Earth and uses its resources has a responsibility to try and prevent environmental damage. Alternatively, may suggest that new technologies will be able to prevent damage.

Pages 25-28 — Mixed Questions — Chemistry 1a

Q1 a)

b) The following should be ticked:
Metals are generally strong but also malleable.
Metals are shiny when freshly cut or polished.
Properties of a metal can be altered by mixing it with another metal to form an alloy.
c) Metals have a giant metallic structure which is held together with metallic bonds. Electrons from the outer shell of each atom can move freely throughout the structure (a 'sea' of electrons). These free electrons can carry electric current.
d) R. The material needs to be as light and as strong as possible with a high melting point and a reasonable price. S has a low melting point. T is expensive and fairly dense. U is not very strong and has a high density.
Q2 a) e.g. lubricants
b) You could get oil spills, which damage the environment.
Q3 a) A finite resource is a resource of which there's a limited amount, which cannot be replenished.
b) i) In general, the more reactive the metal, the later it was discovered.
ii) Less reactive metals are easier to extract from their ores, for example by reduction with carbon. The least reactive metals are sometimes found uncombined in nature.
c)

metal	name of ore	chemical formula of ore
iron	haematite	Fe_2O_3
aluminium	bauxite	Al_2O_3
copper	malachite / chalcopyrite	$CuCO_3$ / $CuFeS_2$

d) i) iron(III) oxide + **carbon monoxide** → iron + **carbon dioxide**
ii) $Fe_2O_3 + 3CO \rightarrow 2Fe + 3CO_2$
e) i) Electrolysis produces very pure copper which conducts better.
ii) Any two of the following: easily bent; ductile/easily drawn into wires; high melting point; good conductor of electricity.
f) Aluminium is more reactive than carbon, and so cannot be extracted by reduction with carbon.
Q4 a) The following can be in any order:
Petrol has a lower melting and boiling point than diesel. Petrol is more volatile (evaporates more easily) than diesel. Petrol is more flammable (ignites more easily) than diesel. Petrol is less viscous (flows more easily / is runnier) than diesel.
b) i) E.g. By the fermentation of plants / hydration of ethene.
ii) When it's burnt, there are fewer pollutants than from petrol or diesel.
Q5 a) Ace oil
b) The viscosity becomes much less.
c) Do the experiment at the average temperature of a car engine.
d) Duncan XYZ oil
Q6 a) i)

common name	limestone	+HEAT (A)	quicklime	+WATER (B)	slaked lime
chemical name	calcium carbonate	→	calcium oxide	→	calcium hydroxide
formula	$CaCO_3$		CaO		$Ca(OH)_2$

ii) $CaCO_3 \rightarrow CaO + CO_2$
iii) E.g. neutralising acid soils in fields / acidity in lakes.
b)

Limestone → (heat with clay) → cement → (add sand, water and gravel) → concrete
Limestone → (heat with sand and sodium carbonate) → glass

c) Any two of: it doesn't rot when it gets wet; it's cheaper; it's fire resistant; it can't be gnawed away be insects or rodents.
d) i) sand and soda / sodium carbonate
ii) The ingredients are heated together until they melt, then they're cooled.
e) Acid rain reacts with the limestone and causes it to dissolve.

Chemistry 1b — Oils, Earth and Atmosphere

Page 29 — Cracking Crude Oil

Q1 shorter, petrol, diesel, long, high, catalyst, molecules, cracking
Q2 a) E.g. petrol, paraffin, ethene
b) too thick (viscous), don't burn easily
c) thermal decomposition
Q3 a) ethene
b) 1. The long-chain molecules are heated.
2. They are vaporised (turned into a gas).
3. The vapour is passed over a catalyst at a high temperature.
4. The molecules are cracked on the surface of the catalyst.
Q4 a) kerosene → octane + ethene
b) $C_{10}H_{22} \rightarrow C_8H_{18} + C_2H_4$

Page 30 — Alkenes and Ethanol

Q1 a) C_2H_4
b) H₂C=CH₂ (structural formula showing C=C double bond with two H atoms on each carbon)

Chemistry 1b — Oils, Earth and Atmosphere

c) Propene

d)
$$H_2C=CH-CH_3$$ (with all H's shown)

e) Two structures showing H−C−C−C=C−H variants with hydrogens

Q2 a) C_5H_{10}
b) C_6H_{12}
c) C_8H_{16}
d) $C_{12}H_{24}$

Q3 a) False
b) True
c) False
d) True

Q4 a) A
b) Any two, in any order:
Needs lower temperatures so is cheaper. Can use simpler equipment. Uses sugar which is often grown as a major crop. Yeast is easy to grow.
c) The ethanol produced is not very concentrated/needs to be purified.
d) High temperature (about 300 °C), high pressure (about 70 atm), phosphoric acid catalyst.

Pages 31-32 — Using Alkenes to Make Polymers

Q1 The monomer of poly(ethene) is ethene.

Q2 a) Different temperatures and pressures of polymerisation. Presence or absence of a catalyst.
b) They are made from different monomers.

Q3 a) Waste remains in landfill. Landfill sites are getting full and more are needed, which takes up useful land.
b) Recycle and reuse.
c) Plastic is currently made from crude oil. As this runs low, its price will rise.

Q4
$$n\begin{pmatrix} CH_3 & H \\ | & | \\ C=C \\ | & | \\ H & H \end{pmatrix} \longrightarrow \begin{pmatrix} CH_3 & H \\ | & | \\ C-C \\ | & | \\ H & H \end{pmatrix}_n$$

Q5 Cracking is the breakdown of large molecules into smaller ones, whereas polymerisation is small molecules joining to form bigger molecules. Cracking makes small alkenes and alkanes, polymerisation often uses alkenes to make alkanes. Cracking usually involves breaking single bonds between carbon atoms. In polymerisation, the double bonds in carbon atoms are broken.

Q6 a) B. Slime made with more concentrated sodium tetraborate solution is more viscous and would flow more slowly.
b) E.g. mass of slime samples used, size of discs, temperature.

Page 33 — Plant Oils and Emulsions

Q1 a) Fruits: e.g. avocados and olives
Seeds: e.g. brazil nuts and sesame seeds
b) e.g. food or fuel
c) It squeezes the oil out of the plant material.
d) It separates the oil from the rest of the plant material.

Q2 a) Vegetable oils provide loads of energy, and also contain nutrients like vitamin E and essential fatty acids.
b) Emulsions can be formed from oil suspended in water or water suspended in oil.
c) The thicker an emulsion, the more oil it contains.
d) Emulsions can be combined with air and it makes them fluffier.
e) Emulsions are found in foods as well as in non-food items such as moisturisers, paints, etc.

Q3 Diagrams showing Milk, Single cream, and Double cream with water and oil droplets (increasing oil content from milk to double cream).

Pages 34-35 — Extracting and Using Plant Oils

Q1 a) E.g. rapeseed oil and soybean oil
b) They provide lots of energy.

Q2 $0.9 \times 37\,000\,000 = 33\,300\,000$ J or 33.3 MJ

Q3 a) Burning biodiesel produces no net increase in carbon dioxide. It produces less sulfur dioxide pollution/particulates. Biodegradable and less toxic. Conserves crude oil, a non-renewable resource.
b) We can't make enough of it, or it costs more to make so it tends to be more expensive.
c) Two from: Biodiesel can be used in diesel car engines without the engine being modified. Biodiesel can use existing filling stations and pumps. Biodiesel is less flammable. Biodiesel doesn't have to be kept under pressure. (Other answers are possible too).

Q4 a) When burnt, biodiesel does produce carbon dioxide, but as it comes from recently grown plants which took in this carbon dioxide during their lives it does not increase the net level of the gas in the atmosphere.
b) Normal diesel is produced from crude oil, the remains of dead plants and animals from millions of years ago. When burnt it produces a net increase in the level of atmospheric carbon dioxide.

Q5 a) Recycled cooking oil
b) Climate change might slow down. Spills would be less harmful to the environment.
c) It has reduced the tax on biodiesel and increased the tax on normal diesel.
d) The Government would get less money from fuel tax. It would have to make cuts in other places (e.g. education) or raise the tax on something else.
e) You don't need to get a diesel car modified. Biodiesel may cost slightly more but the Government is actually making less money on it than it does on normal diesel.

Page 36 — Using Plant Oils

Q1 Martin has produced the better method. It is a fair test. He gives accurate quantities. He labels his equipment so there is no opportunity for mistakes.

Chemistry 1b — Oils, Earth and Atmosphere

Q2 Saturated animal fat — bottom diagram
Polyunsaturated grape seed oil — top diagram
Monounsaturated olive oil — middle diagram

Q3 a) Reaction with hydrogen with a nickel catalyst at about 60 °C. The double bonds open up and bond to the hydrogen atoms.
b) It increases the melting points of vegetable oils.

Q4 a) They increase the amount of cholesterol in the blood, which can block arteries and lead to a heart attack.
b) They increase the amount of bad cholesterol and reduce the amount of good cholesterol.

Pages 37-38 — Food Additives

Q1 a) Chromatography.
b) A
c) A less soluble dye would travel more slowly.

Q2 preserve, additives, chemical, compounds, salt, longer, appearance (or taste), taste (or appearance), E-numbers, sodium sorbate, approved, ingredients.

Q3 a) Wet/dissolve the sweet and transfer some of the colour onto a pencil baseline on a piece of chromatography paper. Put the paper in a beaker of solvent (keep the baseline horizontal and above the solvent). After a given amount of time, measure the distance the dye/s have travelled.
b) Blue has 2 dyes.
c) Brown, because the same pattern of dyes are present.

Q4 Not all additives are synthetic. Some are of natural origin, and other synthetic substances are identical to natural compounds.

Q5 a) Water, as this is listed first.
b) To improve its taste and appearance.
c) Yes, as it uses artificial sweeteners instead of sugar.
d) Carboxymethylcellulose

Pages 39-40 — Plate Tectonics

Q1 continental drift, fossils, South America, South Africa (alternative pairs of places are possible), land bridges, Pangaea, rotation.

Q2 False, True, True, False, True, False, False, False, True, True

Q3 Fossils of identical plants and animals were found on either side of the Atlantic.
The coastlines of South America and South Africa seem to match.
Rocks with matching layers have been found on different continents.
Tropical plant fossils were found in the Arctic islands.

Q4 a) i) Tidal forces and the rotation of the Earth.
ii) The forces would have to be so great that they would stop the Earth from turning, which they hadn't/The forces he proposed were not strong enough.
iii) Two from: He wasn't a qualified geologist. He had used flawed data. His idea just sounded so strange.
b) The ocean floors and mountains.

Pages 41-42 — The Earth's Structure

Q1 a) 1.6 × 10 000 = 16 000 cm = 0.16 km
b) 1.6 × 20 000 = 32 000 cm = 0.32 km
0.32 km + 325 km = 325.32 km

Q2 The main earthquake zones are along the plate boundaries.

Q3 A sphere showing 3 layers.
Labels: Crust (outer layer) — very thin, average 20 km thickness.
Mantle (next layer down) — properties of a solid but flows very slowly like a liquid. Radioactive decay takes place here.
Core (centre) — mostly iron and nickel.

Q4 Crust — Thinnest of the Earth's layers
Mantle — Slowly flowing semi-solid layer that plates float on
Convection current — Caused by radioactive decay in the mantle
Tectonic plates — Large pieces of crust and upper mantle
Eurasian Plate — Moving away from the North American Plate but toward the African Plate
Earthquakes — Caused by sudden movements of plates
Volcanoes — Hot spots that often sit on plate boundaries.
San Andreas Fault — A well-known plate boundary in North America

Q5 Earthquake: Evidence — Strain in underground rocks. How reliable is it? — Can only suggest the possibility of an earthquake. Low reliability.
Volcanic eruption: Evidence — Rising molten rock causing the ground to bulge slightly, leading to mini-earthquakes.
How reliable is it? — Molten rock can cool instead of erupting, so not a definite sign. Low/medium reliability.

Pages 43-46 — The Evolution of the Atmosphere

Q1 True statements: When the Earth was formed, its surface was molten.
When some plants died and were buried under layers of sediment, the carbon they had removed from the atmosphere became locked up as fossil fuels.

Q2 The percentage of carbon dioxide has decreased by a large amount because it dissolved into the oceans and green plants used it for photosynthesis.

Q3 The statements should be in this order (from the top of the timeline):
1. The atmosphere is about four-fifths nitrogen and one-fifth oxygen.
2. More complex organisms evolved.
3. Oxygen built up due to photosynthesis, and the ozone layer developed.
4. Plant life appeared.
5. Water vapour condensed to form oceans.
6. The Earth cooled down slightly. A thin crust formed.
7. The Earth formed. There was lots of volcanic activity.

Q4 a) Largest sector is Nitrogen, second largest is Oxygen, smallest is Carbon dioxide and other gases.
b) Nitrogen: 80% approx (to be more precise, it's 78% in dry air)
Oxygen: 20% approx (to be more precise, it's 21% in dry air)
c) Nitrogen has increased. Carbon dioxide has decreased. Far less water vapour now. Oxygen is now a significant proportion of the atmosphere.
d) As the planet cooled, the water vapour condensed and formed the oceans.
e) Plants and microorganisms photosynthesised and produced it.
f) In any order:
Created the ozone layer which blocked harmful rays from the Sun.
Killed off early organisms/allowed more complex ones to evolve.

Q5 a) helium, neon, argon, krypton, xenon, radon

Chemistry 2(i) — Bonding and Reactions

- b) 0 (or 8)
- c) They are very unreactive and exist as individual atoms.
- d) About 1%
- e) Argon: e.g. used in light bulbs,
  Neon: e.g. used in electric discharge tubes (fluorescent lights)
  Helium: e.g. used in party balloons/airships
- Q6 The water from comets has a higher proportion of "heavy" water than the water found on Earth.
- Q7 a) The ozone layer protects us from harmful UV radiation which causes skin cancer.
- b) No. The rise could also be due to, e.g., more people sunbathing or taking holidays in hot countries.
- Q8 a) Antarctica, and to a lesser extent the Arctic
- b) CFCs
- c) E.g. fridges and aerosol cans
- Q9 a) i) Burning fossil fuels and deforestation (any order)
  ii) Carbon dioxide increases and decreases naturally over millions of years, so what is happening now is not necessarily unusual.
- b) i) Generally increased, although it has fluctuated.
  ii) Greenhouse gases

Pages 47-49 — Mixed Questions — Chemistry 1b

- Q1 a) There are twice as many hydrogen atoms as there are carbon atoms in each molecule (and no other atoms).
- b) E.g.
  $$H-\overset{H}{\underset{H}{C}}-\overset{H}{\underset{H}{C}}-\overset{H}{C}=\overset{H}{C}-\overset{H}{\underset{H}{C}}-H$$
  (The double bond can be between any adjacent carbons.)
- c) Alkanes have no double C=C bond but alkenes do. (The general formula of an alkane is C_nH_{2n+2}.)
- Q2 a) cracking
- b) E.g. decane → propene + heptane
  $C_{10}H_{22} \rightarrow C_3H_6 + C_7H_{16}$
- c) Ethene can be reacted with steam to produce ethanol. This requires a high temperature, high pressure and a catalyst e.g. (phosphoric acid).
- d) Ethanol can be made by fermentation. The advantage of this is that the raw materials used are renewable.
- Q3 a) Lots of small molecules (monomers) join up to make long chain molecules (polymers).
- b) Name: polystyrene / poly(styrene)
- c) E.g. it's difficult to get rid of them.
- Q4 a) i) It's a colouring to make it look more appetising.
  ii) The conclusion is not valid. Only two subjects reported symptoms, which is not enough to draw a valid conclusion. Also, ingredients other than additives could have caused the headaches.
- b) i) Cheddar cheese.
  ii) E.g. heart disease.
- c) i) The molecules have one double bond in their carbon chains.
  ii) Rapeseed oil will decolourise bromine water.
  iii) E.g. mayonnaise, salad dressing, milk, cream, ice cream.
- Q5 a) E.g. it is difficult to gather evidence as you can't see clearly what is happening. The changes which provided evidence happen very slowly. Technological advances have only recently made it possible to investigate things like the ocean floor.
- b) Convection currents in the mantle.
- c) Earthquakes and volcanoes

- Q6 a) No. There was virtually no oxygen. Living organisms need oxygen to respire and release energy from their food.
- b) Green plants
- c) Increasing, carbon dioxide, burning, reduces, absorbed.
- d) i) Vegetable oil / plant crops.
  ii) The CO_2 released when biodiesel is burnt is the same amount as the CO_2 absorbed by the plants it is made from when they grew.
  iii) E.g. it is too expensive / there aren't enough crops to make enough oil / there isn't enough used vegetable oil available.
- e) i) False, only 1% of the atmosphere is noble gases.
  ii) True
  iii) True
  iv) False, scientists can't predict volcanoes and earthquakes with any accuracy.

Chemistry 2(i) — Bonding and Reactions

Page 50 — Atoms

- Q1 a) neutral
- b) ion
- c) protons, electrons (in either order)
- d) negatively
- Q2

Particle	Mass	Charge
Proton	1	+1
Neutron	1	0
Electron	very small	−1

- Q3 a) nucleus
- b) electron
- c) electron
- d) proton
- e) neutron
- f) proton
- Q4 a) The total number of protons and neutrons in an atom.
- b) The number of protons in an atom.
- c)

Element	Symbol	Mass Number	Number of Protons	Number of Electrons	Number of Neutrons
Sodium	Na	23	11	11	12
Oxygen	O	16	8	8	8
Neon	Ne	20	10	10	10
Calcium	Ca	40	20	20	20

Page 51 — Elements, Compounds and Isotopes

- Q1 a) A = element; B = compound; C = element; D = compound
- b) i) C
  ii) A
  iii) D
  iv) B
- Q2 a) Compounds
- b) completely different to
- c) difficult
- d) a compound, an element
- e) electrons
- Q3 Isotopes, element, protons, neutrons.

Chemistry 2(i) — Bonding and Reactions

Q4 W and Y, because these two atoms have the same number of protons but a different mass number.

Q5 Carbon-14 makes up a certain proportion of all the carbon in living things. It gradually decays into nitrogen, so historians are able measure the proportion of carbon-14 in a sample and calculate how long ago it died.

Page 52 — The Periodic Table

Q1 a) radon and krypton
b) sodium
c) nickel
d) iodine
e) silicon or iodine

Q2 a) true
b) false
c) true
d) false
e) true

Q3 a) The following should be ticked: **A** and **D**
b) Fluorine and chlorine are both in Group VII, so they both contain the same number of electrons in their outer shell. The properties of elements are decided by the number of electrons they have in their outer shell.

Q4

	Alternative Name for Group	Number of Electrons in Outer Shell
Group I	Alkali metals	1
Group VII	Halogens	7
Group 0	Noble gases	8

Pages 53-54 — Electron Shells

Q1 a) i) true
ii) false
iii) false
iv) true
v) false

b) ii) The lowest energy levels are always filled first.
iii) Atoms are most stable when they have full outer shells.
v) Reactive elements have partially filled outer shells.

Q2 E.g. The inner most electron shell should be filled first / there should be two electrons in the inner shell;
The outer shell contains too many electrons, it only holds a maximum of 8 electrons;

Q3 a) 2,2
b) 2,6
c) 2,8,4
d) 2,8,8,2
e) 2,8,3
f) 2,8,8

Q4 a) Noble gases are unreactive elements because they have full outer shells of electrons.
b) Alkali metals are reactive elements, because they have an incomplete outer shell of electrons.

Q5 a) 2,8,7
b) [diagram of Cl electron shell]
c) It's outer shell isn't full (it's keen to get an extra electron).

Q6 a) C b) N c) F d) Na e) Mg f) P g) S h) K i) Ca

Pages 55-56 — Ionic Bonding

Q1 a) true
b) true
c) true
d) false
e) true

Q2 a) Group 1
b) 1
c) +1
d) NaCl

Q3 a) 2
b) 2
c) [diagram showing Mg transferring electrons to O, forming Mg^{2+} and O^{2-}]
d) MgO
e) giant ionic

Q4 a) strong, positive, negative, large
b) Any two of: high boiling point, will dissolve to form solutions that conduct electricity, will conduct electricity when molten.

Q5 BeS, K_2S, BeI_2, KI

Q6 a)

	Conducts electricity?
When solid	No
When dissolved in water	Yes
When molten	Yes

b) When solid, the ions are held tightly in a giant ionic structure so they're unable to move and conduct electricity. When dissolved or molten, the ions are free to move and so can conduct electricity.

Page 57 — Electron Shells and Ions

Q1 a) ions
b) readily
c) rarely
d) cations

Q2 a) i) 1
ii) 2
iii) 1
b) i) 2
ii) 1
iii) 1

Chemistry 2(i) — Bonding and Reactions

Q3 a) Cl [2,8,8]⁻

b) Mg [2,8]⁺⁺

c) O [2,8]⁻⁻

Q4 a) [2,8,8]⁺
b) [2,8,8]⁺⁺
c) [2,8]⁻
d) [2]⁺⁺

Page 58 — Covalent Bonding

Q1 a) true
b) true
c) true
d) false
e) true

Q2

Atom	Carbon	Chlorine	Hydrogen	Nitrogen	Oxygen
Number of electrons needed to fill outer shell	4	1	1	3	2

Q3 a) [H–Cl diagram]
b) [O=O diagram]
c) [H₂O diagram]
d) [NH₃ diagram]
e) [CH₄ diagram]

Q4 Sharing electrons allows both atoms to achieve the stable 'full outer shell' of electrons.

Page 59 — Covalent Substances: Two Kinds

Q1 Diamond — I am used in jewellery; I am the hardest natural substance; My carbon atoms form four covalent bonds.
Graphite — I have layers which move over one another; I am used in pencils; I am the only non-metal which is a good conductor of electricity; My carbon atoms form three covalent bonds.
Silicon dioxide — I am used to make glass; I am known as sand; I am not made from carbon.

Q2 uncharged atoms, strong, high, don't, insoluble

Q3 Any two of: low melting point; low boiling point; usually a gas/liquid at room temperature; doesn't conduct electricity.

Q4 a) Each carbon atom in graphite only forms three covalent bonds. This leaves free electrons to carry electricity.

b) Each carbon atom forms four covalent bonds in a very rigid giant covalent structure.

Pages 60-61 — Metallic Structures

Q1 a) metallic
b) heat, electricity (in either order)
c) malleable / bendy / ductile

Q2 They have electrons that are free to move.

Q3 a) E; very high melting point.
b) A; low density, doesn't react with water (in rain clouds etc.).
c) C; high specific heat capacity, low m.p. so can be used as a liquid.
d) A; low density, fairly high electrical conductivity.

Q4 a) giant ionic
b) giant covalent
c) metallic

Q5

Property	Giant Ionic	Giant Covalent	Simple Molecular	Metallic
High melting and boiling points	✓	✓	✗	✓
Can conduct electricity when solid	✗	✗ except graphite	✗	✓
Can conduct electricity when molten	✓	✗ except graphite	✗	✓

Q6 a) giant ionic; it only conducts electricity when molten and dissolved.
b) giant covalent; high melting point, but doesn't conduct electricity
c) simple molecular; low melting point.
d) metallic; conducts electricity.

Chemistry 2(i) — Bonding and Reactions

Pages 62-63 — New Materials

Q1 a) C_{60}
b) 3
c) Yes, each carbon atom only forms three covalent bonds leaving free electrons that can conduct electricity.

Q2 a) Materials that behave differently depending on the conditions.
b) dyes, temperature, liquids, solid, contract

Q3 a) $1 \div 0.000\,001 = \mathbf{1\,000\,000\ nm}$
b) They have a huge surface area, so individual catalyst molecules could be attached to carbon nanotubes. This gives the catalyst an increased surface area, making it more effective.
c) E.g. you can use them to make sensors to detect one type of molecule and nothing else, for example highly specific sensors for testing water purity.

Q4 a) i) false
  ii) true
  iii) true
b) Nitinol is made from nickel and titanium.
c) It remembers its original shape — so if you bend it too far, you can heat it and it goes back to its 'remembered' shape.
d) e.g. glasses frames

Q5 a) tiny hollow carbon tubes
b) They can conduct electricity. They're very small.
c) They're very strong.

Q6 Building a product molecule-by-molecule either by positioning each molecule exactly where you want it or by starting with a bigger structure and taking bits off it.

Page 64 — Relative Formula Mass

Q1 a) How heavy an atom of an element is compared to an atom of carbon-12.
b) i) 24
  ii) 20
  iii) 16
  iv) 1
  v) 12
  vi) 64
  vii) 39
  viii) 40
  ix) 35.5

Q2 Element A is helium
Element B is $(3 \times 4) = 12 =$ carbon
Element C is $(4 \times 4) = 16 =$ oxygen

Q3 a) You add the relative atomic masses of all the atoms in the compound together.
b) i) $(2 \times 1) + 16 = 18$
  ii) $39 + 16 + 1 = 56$
  iii) $1 + 14 + (3 \times 16) = 63$
  iv) $(2 \times 1) + 32 + (4 \times 16) = 98$
  v) $14 + (4 \times 1) + 14 + (3 \times 16) = 80$

Q4 $2XOH + H_2 = 114$
$2 \times (X + 16 + 1) + (2 \times 1) = 114$
$2 \times (X + 17) + 2 = 114$
$2 \times (X + 17) = 112$
$X + 17 = 56$
$X = 39$
so $X =$ potassium

Page 65 — Two Formula Mass Calculations

Q1 a) Percentage mass of an element in a compound =
$\dfrac{A_r \times \text{No. of atoms (of that element)} \times 100}{M_r \text{ (of whole compound)}}$
b) i) $(14 \times 2) \div [14 + (4 \times 1) + 14 + (3 \times 16)] \times 100 = 35\%$
  ii) $(4 \times 1) \div [14 + (4 \times 1) + 14 + (3 \times 16)] \times 100 = 5\%$
  iii) $(3 \times 16) \div [14 + (4 \times 1) + 14 + (3 \times 16)] \times 100 = 60\%$

Q2 a) $14 \div (14 + 16) \times 100 = 47\%$
b)

	Nitrogen	Oxygen
Percentage mass (%)	30.4	69.6
$\div A_r$	$(30.4 \div 14) = 2.17$	$(69.6 \div 16) = 4.35$
Ratio	1	2

empirical formula = NO_2

Q3

	Calcium	Oxygen	Hydrogen
Mass (g)	0.8	0.64	0.04
$\div A_r$	$(0.8 \div 40) = 0.02$	$(0.64 \div 16) = 0.04$	$(0.04 \div 1) = 0.04$
Ratio	1	2	2

empirical formula = $Ca(OH)_2$ (or CaO_2H_2)

Q4 a) A = $(3 \times 16) \div [(2 \times 56) + (3 \times 16)] \times 100 = 30\%$
B = $16 \div [(2 \times 1) + 16)] \times 100 = 88\%$
C = $(3 \times 16) \div [40 + 12 + (3 \times 16)] \times 100 = 48\%$
b) B

Pages 66-67 — Calculating Masses in Reactions

Q1 a) $2Mg + O_2 \rightarrow 2MgO$
b)
2Mg   2MgO
$2 \times 24 = 48$ $2 \times (24 + 16) = 80$
$48 \div 48 = 1$ g $80 \div 48 = 1.67$ g
$1 \times 10 = 10$ g $1.67 \times 10 = \mathbf{16.7\ g}$

Q2
4Na $2Na_2O$
$4 \times 23 = 92$ $2 \times [(2 \times 23) + 16] = 124$
$92 \div 124 = 0.74$ g $124 \div 124 = 1$ g
$0.74 \times 2 = \mathbf{1.5\ g}$ $1 \times 2 = 2$ g

Q3 a) $2Al + Fe_2O_3 \rightarrow Al_2O_3 + 2Fe$
b)
Fe_2O_3 2Fe
$[(2 \times 56) + (3 \times 16)] = 160$ $2 \times 56 = 112$
$160 \div 160 = 1$ g $112 \div 160 = 0.7$
$1 \times 20 = 20$ g $0.7 \times 20 = \mathbf{14\ g}$

Q4 $CaCO_3 \rightarrow CaO + CO_2$
$CaCO_3$ CaO
$40 + 12 + (3 \times 16) = 100$ $40 + 16 = 56$
$100 \div 56 = 1.786$ kg $56 \div 56 = 1$ kg
$1.786 \times 100 = \mathbf{178.6\ kg}$ $1 \times 100 = 100$ kg

Q5 a)
C   2CO
12                 $2 \times (12 + 16) = 56$
$12 \div 12 = 1$ g $56 \div 12 = 4.67$ g
$1 \times 10 = 10$ g $4.67 \times 10 = 46.7$ g
46.7 g of CO is produced in stage B — all this is used in stage C.
3CO $3CO_2$
$3 \times (12 + 16) = 84$ $3 \times [12 + (2 \times 16)] = 132$
$84 \div 84 = 1$ g $132 \div 84 = 1.57$ g
$1 \times 46.7 = 46.7$ g $1.57 \times 46.7 = \mathbf{73.3\ g}$
b) It could be recycled and used in stage B.

Chemistry 2(ii) — Rates of Reaction

Q6 a) 2NaOH + H$_2$SO$_4$ → Na$_2$SO$_4$ + 2H$_2$O
b)
2NaOH   Na$_2$SO$_4$
2 × (23 + 16 + 1) = 80   (2 × 23) + 32 + (4 × 16) = 142
80 ÷ 142 = 0.56 g   142 ÷ 142 = 1 g
0.56 × 75 = **42 g**   1 × 75 = 75 g
c)
H$_2$SO$_4$ 2H$_2$O
(2 × 1) + 32 + (4 × 16) = 98   2 × [(2 × 1) + 16] = 36
98 ÷ 98 = 1 g   36 ÷ 98 = 0.37 g
1 × 50 = 50 g   0.37 × 50 = **18.5 g**

Pages 68-69 — The Mole

Q1 a) mass, relative formula mass
b) i) 64 g
ii) 3 × (2 × 35.5) = 213 g
iii) 2 × [1 + 14 + (16 × 3)] = 126 g
iv) 0.5 × [40 + 12 + (16 × 3)] = 50 g
Q2 a) 24 litres
b) i) 4.5 × 24 = 108 litres
ii) 2.4 × 24 = 57.6 litres
iii) 0.48 × 24 = 11.52 litres
Q3 a) number of moles = volume × moles per litre
b) i) 2 × 0.05 = 0.1 moles
ii) 0.5 × 0.25 = 0.125 moles
iii) 1.75 × 0.55 = 0.9625 moles
c) moles per litre = no. of moles ÷ volume
= 0.25 ÷ 0.2
= 1.25 M
d) volume = no. of moles ÷ moles per litre
= 2 ÷ 1.5
= 1.3 litres
Q4 a) number of moles = $\frac{\text{mass in g}}{M_r}$
b) i) 20 ÷ 40 = 0.5 moles
ii) 112 ÷ 32 = 3.5 moles
iii) 200 ÷ (64 + 16) = 2.5 moles
c) i) 2 × 23 = 46 g
ii) 0.75 × (24 + 16) = 30 g
iii) 0.025 × [207 + (35.5 × 2)] = 6.95 g
Q5 a) no. of moles = mass ÷ A_r
= 13 ÷ 65
= 0.2 moles
b) 2 × 0.2 = 0.4 moles
Q6 a) Mg + H$_2$SO$_4$ → MgSO$_4$ + H$_2$
b) number of moles of magnesium = 0.6 ÷ 24 = 0.025
number of moles of hydrogen produced = 0.025
volume of hydrogen produced = 0.025 × 24 = 0.6 litres
c) number of moles of MgSO$_4$ formed = 0.025
0.025 × [24 + 32 + (16 × 4)] = 3 g

Page 70 — Atom Economy

Q1 a) copper
b) M_r CuO = 64 + 16 = 80
(2 × 64) ÷ [(2 × 64) + 12] × 100 = 74%
c) 100 − 74 = 26%
Q2 a) Reactions with a high atom economy use up their resources less rapidly and produce less water. This lowers the cost of disposing the water safely, and is cheaper as the raw resources can often be very expensive. This all means a higher profit.

b) Reactions that only have one product, e.g. the Haber process.
Q3 a) M_r TiCl$_4$ = (48 + (4 × 35.5)) = 190
With magnesium: 48 ÷ [190 + (2 ÷ 24)] × 100 = 20.2%
With sodium: 48 ÷ [190 + (4 × 23)] × 100 = 17%
b) The method with magnesium has the best atom economy.
Q4 Cr$_2$O$_3$ + 2Al → Al$_2$O$_3$ + 2Cr
M_r Cr$_2$O$_3$ = (2 × 52) + (3 × 16) = 152
(2 × 52) ÷ [152 + (2 × 27)] × 100 = 50.5%

Page 71 — Percentage Yield

Q1 a) percentage yield = $\frac{\text{actual yield}}{\text{predicted yield}} \times 100$
b) 1.2 ÷ 2.7 × 100 = 44.4%
Q2 a) Not all the reactants are turned into products.
b) Some of the liquid remains with the solid and filter paper, and in the original container.
c) Some of the liquid remains on the inside surface of the old container.
d) The reactants form an unexpected product.
Q3 a) 6 ÷ 15 × 100 = 40%
b) When they transferred the solid to a clean piece of filter paper, some of the solid would have remained on the filter paper; some of the solid may have remained in the liquid during filtration.

Pages 72-73 — Mixed Questions — Chemistry 2(i)

Q1 a) R = graphite; S = diamond; T = buckminsterfullerene
b) i) They both have a giant covalent structure. All the atoms are bonded to each other by strong covalent bonds in a giant network. It therefore requires lots of energy to separate the carbon atoms.
ii) It will have a lower melting point than form R or S. It does not have a giant covalent structure. The structure is simple molecular, with relatively weak forces between C$_{60}$ molecules.
Q2 a)

	Silicon	Chlorine
Mass (g)	1.4	7.1
÷ A_r	(1.4 ÷ 28) = 0.05	(7.1 ÷ 35.5) = 0.2
Ratio	1	4

Empirical formula = **SiCl$_4$**
b) (35.5 × 4) ÷ [(35.5 × 4) + 28] × 100 = **83.5%**
c) Si + 2Cl$_2$ → SiCl$_4$
d) 6.5 ÷ 8.5 × 100 = 76%
e) Yes, there's only one product, so the atom economy is 100%.
Q3 a) Ca atom: [2,8,8,2]
Ca^{2+} ion: [2,8,8]$^{2+}$
b) 20
c) Any of: beryllium, magnesium, strontium, barium, radium.

Chemistry 2(ii) — Rates of Reaction

Q4 a) A / B / F. Simple molecular substances have weak intermolecular forces and therefore low melting and boiling points. They do not conduct electricity since they don't consist of ions or have free electrons.
b) C
c) All metals are good conductors of electricity when solid. / Substance D is a poor conductor of electricity when solid.

Q5 a) 24 + [2 × (14 + 16 × 3)] = 148
b) i) Mg: 0.12 ÷ 24 = 0.005 mol
Mg(NO$_3$)$_2$: 0.74 ÷ 148 = 0.005 mol
ii) 0.005 ÷ 0.2 = 0.025 mol/dm^3
c) 0.025 × [1 + 14 + (16 × 3)] = 1.575 g

Chemistry 2(ii) — Rates of Reaction

Page 74 — Rates of Reaction

Q1 a) higher
b) lower
c) gases, faster
d) increases
e) isn't

Q2 a) i) Z
ii) It has the steepest gradient.
b) So that all the marble reacts/is used up.
c) Equal masses of marble chips were used each time.
d) The curve should be steeper and show that a larger volume of gas is produced, e.g. like this:

Q3 a) decrease
b) More reactant was used.
c) The reactants in Q might be in smaller pieces/have a larger surface area/be more concentrated/be at a higher temperature.

Pages 75-76 — Measuring Rates of Reaction

Q1 a) speed, reactants, formed.
b) precipitation, faster.
c) gas, mass, volume.

Q2 a) C
b) i) Point K: 0.08 ÷ 5 = 0.016 g/s
ii) Point L: 0.06 ÷ 15 = 0.004 g/s

Q3 a) 94
64
45.5
35
9
b) 50 in the third column of the table should be circled.
c) 2 mol/dm^3

d) i) Gas syringe
ii) Stopwatch/stopclock/timer/balance/measuring cylinder
e) Sketch should look something like this:

f) To improve reliability of results
g) Bad experimental technique, e.g. misreading value from gas syringe, not emptying gas syringe before starting.
h) Any 2 reasonable suggestions, e.g., take more readings for each concentration, use more concentrations, improve dilution technique.

Pages 77-80 — Rate of Reaction Experiments

Q1 increase, faster, surface area, react.
Q2 a) B
b) Curve should be between curves A and B. It should level off at same height.
c) CO$_2$ + CaCl$_2$
d) Size of marble pieces.
e) No, you cannot tell if it was a fair test. The same mass of marble chips was used each time but it is not known if the same volume of HCl was used each time or if the temperature was kept constant.
f) Counting how many bubbles are produced per minute.
Measuring how quickly the reaction loses mass.

Q3 a) 13 (he took one at the start).
b) x-axis: time (s)
y-axis: change/loss in mass (g)
c)

d) 145.73 − 143.89 = 1.84 g

Q4 a) 1, because the slope of the graph is steepest.
b)

c) The reactions finish eventually / the reagent(s) are always used up eventually.

Chemistry 2(ii) — Rates of Reaction

Q5   All the reactants are soluble.
The precipitate is yellow.
The mixture goes cloudy.
Q6 a)   conical flask, water bath, stopclock, thermometer.
   b) i) Faster
     ii) 145 s
   c) i) Temperature.
     ii) Time taken for cross to disappear.
   d) Repeat the investigation to get more results and find the average for each temperature.
Q7   Increasing the concentration of HCl increases the rate of reaction.
Q8 a) The compound breaks down into simpler substances.
   b) $2H_2O$
   c) C
   d) increase, decomposition, manganese (IV) oxide.
Q9 a) Volume of gas (cm^3/dm^3/l/ml)
   b) R
   c) Reaction R has the steepest graph, so it is the fastest reaction and so must have used the most effective catalyst.

Page 81 — Collision Theory

Q1   increasing the temperature — makes the particles move faster, so they collide more often
decreasing the concentration — means fewer particles of reactants are present, so fewer collisions occur
adding a catalyst — provides a surface for particles to stick to and lowers activation energy
increasing the surface area — gives particles a bigger area of solid reactant to react with
Q2 a) energy
   b) faster, more
   c) rate of reaction.
Q3 a) i) increase
     ii) The particles are closer together so there's more chance of successful collisions.
   b) [diagram showing low pressure and high pressure]

Q4 a) False
   b) True
   c) False
   d) True
Q5   Increase

Page 82 — Catalysts

Q1 a) activation energy.
   b) A
   c) [energy diagram showing curves B and A with activation energy (without catalyst) and activation energy (with catalyst), Reactants and Products labelled, Progress of Reaction on x-axis]

Q2 a) E.g. powder
   b) To give them a large surface area.
   c) They give the reacting particles a surface to stick to and increase the number of successful collisions by lowering the activation energy.
   d) They can be expensive to buy, they need to be removed and cleaned, they can be poisoned by impurities and stop working.
Q3 a) Transition metals.
   b) e.g. nickel is used for cracking hydrocarbons, iron is used in the Haber process.
Q4   CO reacts very slowly with air to form CO_2. Before this happens it can be inhaled by people. The catalyst speeds up the reaction so most of the CO is converted to CO_2 before the gases even pass out of the exhaust.

Pages 83-84 — Energy Transfer in Reactions

Q1   give out, heat, rise, temperature.
Q2 a) N, B, N, B.
   b) combustion
   c) methane + oxygen → carbon dioxide + water
or ethanol + oxygen → carbon dioxide + water
Q3   take in, heat, fall/decrease, temperature.
Q4 a) $CaCO_3 \rightarrow CaO + CO_2$
   b) i) endothermic
     ii) Because the reaction takes in heat.
   c) i) 1 800 000 ÷ 1000 = 1800 kJ
     ii) 90 000 ÷ 1 800 000 = 0.05 tonnes or 50 kg
Q5 a) When he dropped water on it / when it turned blue / the second part.
   b) When he heated up the copper sulphate / the first part.
   c) hydrated.
   d) Left-hand side is blue, right-hand side is white.
Q6 a) X
   b) N
   c) X
   d) N

Pages 85-86 — Reversible Reactions

Q1 a) products, react, reactants
   b) balance
   c) closed, escape
Q2 a) i) A, B
     ii) AB
   b) i) Y
     ii) X
   c) $A + B \rightleftharpoons AB$
   d) At the same rate.
Q3 a) True
   b) False
   c) True
   d) False
Q4 a) Temperature, pressure.
   b) It must be endothermic, so it takes in heat.
   c) backward
   d) All reversible reactions are exothermic in one direction and endothermic in the other, so temperature will always change the position of equilibrium.
   e) It will have no effect because both sides of the reaction have the same number of molecules / volume.

Chemistry 2(iii) — Using Ions in Solution

Q5 a) i) Forward, because there are three molecules on the left-hand side of the reaction and only two molecules on the right-hand side of the reaction.
  ii) It moves it to the right / increases the amount of SO_3 produced.
b) B
c) It stays the same.

Page 87 — The Haber Process

Q1 a) i) Nitrogen and hydrogen.
  ii) The left-hand side.
b) E.g. fertiliser / explosives / dyestuffs
Q2 a) 200 atmospheres, 450°C.
b) 1. High enough to give a good % yield.
  2. Not so high that the plant becomes too expensive to build.
Q3 a) The higher the temperature the less ammonia will be formed.
b) To increase the rate of reaction.
c) They are recycled.
Q4 a) It has no effect on % yield.
b) It would make it cheaper to produce. The rate of reaction is increased without an expensive increase in temperature. Ammonia can be made in a relatively short space of time, meaning lower running costs for the same amount of ammonia produced.

Pages 88-89 — Mixed Questions — Chemistry 2(ii)

Q1 a) Increasing the temperature.
Increasing the concentration of the reactants (or the pressure).
Adding a catalyst.
Increasing the surface area of solid reactants.
b) Measuring the change in mass of the reactants using a mass balance.
Measuring the volume of gas given off with a gas syringe.
Measuring the time it takes for a mark to disappear for a precipitation reaction.
Q2 a) Q
b) R
c) Measure the volume of gas given off using a gas syringe.
Q3 a) True
b) True
c) False. An explosion is an example of a fast reaction.
d) True
e) True
Q4 a) An exothermic reaction is one which gives out energy to the surroundings, (usually in the form of heat and usually shown by a rise in temperature).
b) Exothermic
c) i) Endothermic
  ii) E.g. hydrated copper sulfate, calcium carbonate.
d) If you increase the temperature you increase the forward reaction.
If you decrease the temperature you increase the reverse reaction.

Q5 a) $N_2 + 3H_2 \rightleftharpoons 2NH_3$
b) i) increase, lowering, lower
  ii) This increases their surface area and so increases the rate of reaction.
c) i) The higher the pressure, the greater the number of collisions between the particles.
  ii) Increase
  iii) If you raise the pressure it encourages the reaction that produces less volume. The forward reaction produces less volume.
d) Decrease

Chemistry 2(iii) — Using Ions in Solution

Pages 90-91 — Acids and Alkalis

Q1 a) acid + base → **salt + water**
b) neutralisation
c) i) H^+(aq) and OH^-(aq)
  ii) H^+(aq)
  iii) OH^-(aq)
  iv) Na^+(aq) and Cl^-(aq)
  v) OH^-(aq)
  vi) H^+(aq)
Q2 a) i) [graph: pH vs Number of tablets, rising from pH 1 to pH 9]
  ii) The pH increases from pH 1 to pH 9. It increases most sharply between pH 3 and pH 7.
  iii) 3
b) E.g. the new line should be above the previous one and reach pH 7 at 2 tablets.
[graph with new line added]

Q3 a) i) alkali
  ii) OH^-
  iii) H^+
b) neutralises, increases, acid, acidic, lime/alkali.
Q4 a) Test the solution with universal indicator or a pH meter.
b) Baking soda or soap powder, because they are weak bases and so would neutralise the acid but wouldn't irritate or harm the skin. Stronger bases like caustic soda might damage the skin.
c) The colour can be difficult to judge exactly / Dyes can't give an exact reading, only a general idea / other answers are possible.
Q5 a) neutral
b) dyes
c) 7
d) hydrochloric acid

155

Chemistry 2(iii) — Using Ions in Solution

Pages 92-93 — Acids Reacting with Metals

Q1 a)

Labels: sulfuric acid, hydrogen, aluminium

b) aluminium + **sulfuric acid** → aluminium sulfate + **hydrogen**
c) $2Al + 3H_2SO_4 \rightarrow Al_2(SO_4)_3 + 3H_2$
d) zinc + sulfuric acid → zinc sulfate + hydrogen
e) i) $Mg + 2HCl \rightarrow MgCl_2 + H_2$
   ii) $Ca + 2HNO_3 \rightarrow Ca(NO_3)_2 + H_2$

Q2 a) A
b) B
c) A, C and D
d) A: magnesium
   B: copper
   C: iron
   D: zinc

Q3 a) For example, the number of gas bubbles produced in a certain time / the time it takes for the metal to disappear completely / the volume of gas produced in a certain time / loss of mass in a certain time.
b) acid concentration
c) Two from: volume of acid, the mass / size of the metal pieces, temperature.

Q4 metals, hydrogen, silver, reactive, more, chlorides, sulfuric, nitric.

Q5 a) i) $Ca + 2HCl \rightarrow CaCl_2 + H_2$
ii) $2Na + 2HCl \rightarrow 2NaCl + H_2$
iii) $2Li + H_2SO_4 \rightarrow Li_2SO_4 + H_2$
b) i) magnesium bromide
ii) $2Al + 6HBr \rightarrow 2AlBr_3 + 3H_2$

Pages 94-95 — Oxides, Hydroxides and Ammonia

Q1 a) hydrochloric acid + lead oxide → **lead** chloride + **water**
b) nitric acid + copper hydroxide → copper **nitrate** + water
c) sulfuric acid + zinc oxide → zinc sulfate + **water**
d) hydrochloric acid + **nickel** oxide → nickel **chloride** + **water**
e) **nitric** acid + copper oxide → **copper** nitrate + **water**
f) sulfuric acid + **sodium** hydroxide → sodium **sulfate** + **water**

Q2 a) The following should be ticked:
Acids react with metal oxides to form a salt and water.
Salts and water are formed when acids react with metal hydroxides.
Ammonia solution is alkaline.
b) $H_2SO_4 + CuO \rightarrow CuSO_4 + H_2O$
$HCl + NaOH \rightarrow NaCl + H_2O$

Q3 a) E.g. potassium oxide / hydroxide + sulfuric acid
b) ammonia + hydrochloric acid
c) E.g. silver oxide / hydroxide + nitric acid

Q4 a) NH_3
b) gas, alkaline, nitrogen, proteins, salts, fertilisers
c) ammonia + nitric acid → ammonium nitrate
d) Because it has nitrogen from two sources, the ammonia and the nitric acid.
e) No water is produced.

Q5 a) i) CuO(s)
ii) H_2O(l)
iii) HCl(aq)
iv) ZnO(aq)
v) Na_2SO_4(aq) + H_2O(l)
b) i) $2NaOH + H_2SO_4 \rightarrow Na_2SO_4 + 2H_2O$
ii) $Mg(OH)_2 + 2HNO_3 \rightarrow Mg(NO_3)_2 + 2H_2O$
iii) $2NH_3 + H_2SO_4 \rightarrow (NH_4)_2SO_4$

Pages 96-97 — Making Salts

Q1 a) soluble
b) insoluble
c) insoluble, neutralised
d) precipitation
e) more, less

Q2 a) B
b) D
c) A
d) C

Q3 a) The magnesium displaces the copper from the solution, and the displaced copper coats the piece of magnesium.
b) magnesium sulfate
c) The magnesium isn't in contact with the solution any more, as it is covered with a layer of copper.
d) displacement

Q4 a) **silver nitrate** + **sodium chloride** → silver chloride + **sodium nitrate**
b) The silver chloride must be filtered out of the solution. It needs to be washed and then dried on filter paper / by heating.

Q5 a) a spatula
b) 1. The nickel carbonate no longer dissolves / solid remains in the flask.
2. Bubbles no longer form.
c)

Labels: funnel, nickel carbonate, nickel sulfate solution

d) filtration
e) Heat the nickel sulfate solution to evaporate off the water.

Chemistry 2(iii) — Using Ions in Solution

Page 98 — Electrolysis and the Half-Equations

Q1 a) It could be melted.
b) Cathode: $Pb^{2+} + 2e^- \rightarrow Pb$
Anode: $2Br^- \rightarrow Br_2 + 2e^-$

Q2 a) A: H^+
B: Cl^-
C: H_2
D: Cl_2
b) Cathode: $2H^+ + 2e^- \rightarrow H_2$
Anode: $2Cl^- \rightarrow Cl_2 + 2e^-$

Q3 a) Chlorine gas was produced in the experiment, and it is also used in solution to kill bacteria in swimming pools.
b) Chlorine gas is toxic.
c) The experiment should be carried out in a fume cupboard / The lab should be checked to make sure it is well ventilated.

Q4 Electrolysis is the breaking down of substances using electricity. For electricity to flow, charged ions need to be free to move, and so you need a liquid.

Pages 99-100 — Electrolysis of Salt Water

Q1 a) Hydrogen gas gives a 'squeaky pop' when it comes into contact with a burning splint.
b) Chlorine bleaches damp litmus paper.

Q2 a) chlorine
b) $100 - (11 + 2 + 8 + 11 + 14 + 5 + 6 + 21 + 8) = 14\%$
c) e.g. organic chemicals / oven cleaner
d) plastics

Q3 concentrated, chlorine, disinfectant, plastics, cathode, ammonia/margarine, ammonia/margarine, sodium hydroxide, ceramics/soap, ceramics/soap

Q4 At least 2 of the following points:
Close to power sources, as a lot of electricity will be needed. / Close to the sea as a source of salt water, or to a rock salt mine. / Near to a large enough workforce with relevant skills. / Located in an area where industries that need the products of brine electrolysis are found (e.g. margarine, ceramics, plastics, etc.) / Close to rail or other transport links, to bring in raw materials and to take products away. / Other sensible point.

Q5 The two halves of the electrolysis cell are separated by a diaphragm / membrane that only ions in solution can pass across. Hydrogen gas is only given off at the cathode and chlorine gas is only given off at the anode. This allows the two gases to be piped away separately from the two halves of the electrolysis cell.

Page 101 — Purifying Copper by Electrolysis

Q1 Cathode: $Cu^{2+}(aq) + 2e^- \rightarrow Cu(s)$
Anode: $Cu(s) \rightarrow Cu^{2+}(aq) + 2e^-$

Q2 The impurities are not charged (i.e. they are neutral) so they are not attracted to the cathode.

Q3 a) It is extracted from its ore by reduction with carbon.
b) Copper is often used in electrical conductors, and the purer it is, the better it conducts.
c) impure copper
d) The electrical supply pulls electrons off the atoms of copper at the anode, giving Cu^{2+} ions. These positive ions are attracted to the negative cathode, where the ions get electrons back to make them pure copper atoms, which bind to the cathode.

Q4 Cathode: $Ag^+(aq) + e^- \rightarrow Ag(s)$
Anode: $Ag(s) \rightarrow Ag^+(aq) + e^-$

Q5 The copper produced will have zinc impurities in it.

Pages 102-103 — Mixed Questions — Chemistry 2(iii)

Q1 a) i) acidic
ii) alkaline
b) Milk of magnesia is alkaline, so it can neutralise the excess acid that causes indigestion.

Q2 a) $Mg + 2HCl \rightarrow MgCl_2 + H_2$
b) The pH would increase / it would become less acidic, until it finally reached neutral pH / pH 7 (if there was enough magnesium).
c) Magnesium sulfate.

Q3 a) i) $MgCl_2$
ii) The magnesium oxide would disappear as it reacted.
b) sulfuric acid / H_2SO_4
c) Insoluble.

Q4 You can't simply add an excess of base and then filter to remove it, and you can't just filter out the final product either. You have to add **exactly** the right amount of base, and do a trial experiment using indicator first to find out what this amount is.

Q5 a) i) They gain electrons to become aluminium atoms again.
ii) $Al^{3+} + 3e^- \rightarrow Al$
b) $2O^{2-} \rightarrow O_2 + 2e^-$

Q6 a) A — sodium hydroxide solution
B — hydrogen
C — chlorine
D — sodium ions
E — chloride ions (D and E may be in either order.)
F — diaphragm
b) Chlorine, any from — disinfectants, killing bacteria, plastics, HCl, insecticides.
Hydrogen, any from — making ammonia, margarine, as a fuel.
Sodium hydroxide, any from — soap, ceramics, organic chemicals, paper pulp, oven cleaner.

Q7 a) So it can be used in electrical conductors.
b) Copper ions are positively charged, so they are attracted to the negatively charged cathode.
c) They gain electrons to become atoms again and bind to the cathode.

Chemistry 3(i) — Chemical Concepts

Chemistry 3(i) — Chemical Concepts

Page 104 — History of the Periodic Table

Q1 a) In the modern periodic table, the elements are ordered according to their **atomic number**.
  b) Before this, the known elements were arranged in order according to their **relative atomic mass**.
Q2 a) true
  b) false
  c) true
  d) false
Q3 a) 1
  b) Because he noticed that every eighth element had similar properties.
  c) They hadn't been discovered when Newlands came up with his table.
Q4 a) germanium, 5.32 g/cm³
  b) i) Mendeleev arranged the elements in order of atomic mass and kept elements with similar properties in the same vertical groups, like Newlands.
  ii) Unlike Newlands, Mendeleev left gaps for undiscovered elements.

Pages 105-106 — The Modern Periodic Table

Q1 a) K
  b) Li
  c) K
  d) K
  e) Ar
Q2 a) fluorine, chlorine and iodine / F, Cl and I
  b) helium and argon / He and Ar
  c) iodine / I
Q3 a) The number of outer electrons is the same as the group number.
  b) magnesium = 2, 8, 2
  oxygen = 2, 6
  sulfur = 2, 8, 6
  c) Oxygen is more reactive than sulfur because its outer shell of electrons is closer to the nucleus, so it's less shielded and attracts electrons more strongly.
Q4 a) (electron) shielding
  b) i) The outer electrons are further from the nucleus and are more shielded from the attraction of the nucleus.
  ii) This makes potassium more reactive than lithium.
  c) i) The positive charge of fluorine's nucleus is less shielded by inner shells of electrons than bromine's, and fluorine's outermost shell is closer to the nucleus than bromine's.
  ii) The reactivity decreases down the group because the attraction for electrons decreases.
Q5 a)

  b) Group I

  c) These elements would be less reactive. As you go down a group, elements contain more shells of electrons, so there's increased electron shielding and an increased distance from the nucleus. The outer electron's more easily lost.

Page 107 — Group 1 — The Alkali Metals

Q1 lithium, sodium, potassium
Q2 a) false — they lose electrons to form 1⁺ ions
  b) false
  c) true
  d) true
Q3 soft, sodium hydroxide, hydrogen, electron, positive
Q4 a) They are low compared to most other metals.
  b) The melting point decreases going down the group.
  c) i) increases
  ii) decreases
Q5 a) Lithium is less dense than water.
  b) The solution would turn purple, because lithium hydroxide is formed which is a strong alkali.
  c) $2Li(s) + 2H_2O(l) \rightarrow 2LiOH(aq) + H_2(g)$

Page 108 — Group VII — The Halogens

Q1 bromine — red-brown liquid
  chlorine — green-yellow gas
  fluorine — yellow gas
  iodine — grey solid
Q2 a) false
  b) true
  c) false
  d) true
Q3 The halogens exist as molecules — which are pairs of atoms.
  A more reactive halogen — will displace a less reactive one.
  The halogens react with most metals — forming ionic salts.
  The reactivity of the halogens — decreases as you move down the group.
Q4 a) bromine vapour is a poisonous gas
  b) iron bromide
  c) ionic bonding
Q5 a) Bromine is more reactive than iodine so displaces it from the potassium iodide solution. Bromine is less reactive than chlorine so doesn't displace it from potassium chloride solution.
  b) $Br_2(aq) + 2KI(aq) \rightarrow I_2(aq) + 2KBr(aq)$.

Pages 109-110 — Transition Elements

Q1 in the middle, unreactive, densities, high, good, coloured, catalysts
Q2 a) good conductivity
  b) shiny appearance
  c) 2, 8, 16, 2
Q3 a) iron — ammonia production
  nickel — converting natural oils into fats
  manganese(IV) oxide — decomposition of hydrogen peroxide
  b) i) 2, 8, 14, 2
  ii) 2, 8, 11, 2
  iii) 2, 8, 16, 2

Chemistry 3(i) — Chemical Concepts

c) i) Fe^{2+}, Fe^{3+}
   ii) Cu^+, Cu^{2+}
   iii) Cr^{2+}, Cr^{3+}
Q4 a) You would see green, red-brown and blue coloured crystals.
b) i) 2, 8, 15, 2
   ii) Co^{2+}
   iii) sodium silicate + cobalt chloride → **cobalt silicate + sodium chloride**
Q5 1. Found in the block between Groups II and III of the periodic table.
2. Has a high melting point.
3. Has a high density.
4. Has a shiny appearance.
5. Forms coloured compounds.
6. Forms two different chlorides / forms ions with different charges.

Page 111 — Acids and Alkalis

Q1 a) $H^+(aq)$
b) $OH^-(aq)$
c) $H^+(aq)$
Q2 a) i) When mixed with **water**, all acids release **H^+ / hydrogen** ions.
   ii) When mixed with **water**, all alkalis release **OH^- / hydroxide** ions.
b) Ammonia gas behaved as a base even when it wasn't dissolved in water / ammonia gas does not contain OH^- ions.
c) Charged subatomic particles had not been discovered in the 1880s / scientists didn't realise it was possible to have charged ions at the time.
Q3 a) H^+
b) Lowry and Brønsted
c) When the two gases react, the hydrogen chloride behaves as **an acid** by **donating a proton to the ammonia molecule**.
At the same time the ammonia behaves as **a base** by **accepting a proton from the acid**.
Q4 a) Potassium hydroxide molecules dissociate in water to release hydroxide ions.
b) NH_3 molecules take hydrogen ions from water to give NH_4^+ ions, leaving OH^- ions behind in solution.

Page 112 — Acids, Alkalis and Titration

Q1 a) false
b) true
c) false
d) true
e) false
Q2 a) ...the flask is swirled regularly.
b) ...pink to colourless.
Q3 a) a pH meter
b) a weak acid
c) The concentration of H^+ ions increased.
Q4 a) The independent variable is the fizzy drink used, and the dependent variable is the amount of alkali needed to neutralise it.
b) e.g. phenolphthalein — colourless to pink
c) Kolafizz

Pages 113-114 — Titration Calculations

Q1 a) $2 \times 1 = 2$ moles
b) $1 \times (100 \div 1000) = 0.1$ moles
c) $0.1 \times (25 \div 1000) = 0.0025$ moles
d) $0.2 \times (10 \div 1000) = 0.002$ moles
Q2 a) $HCl + NaOH \rightarrow$ **$NaCl + H_2O$**
b) $H_2SO_4 + Ca(OH)_2 \rightarrow$ **$CaSO_4 + 2H_2O$**
c) $H_2SO_4 + 2 KOH \rightarrow$ **$K_2SO_4 + 2H_2O$**
d) $2 HNO_3 + Ca(OH)_2 \rightarrow$ **$Ca(NO_3)_2 + 2H_2O$**
Q3 a) i) $0.5 \times (23 + 16 + 1) = 20$ g
   ii) $0.2 \times (2 + 32 + 64) = 19.6$ g
   iii) $0.02 \times (40 + 32 + 2) = 1.48$ g
b) i) $0.1 \times (39 + 16 + 1) = 5.6$ g/dm³
   ii) $2 \times (1 + 14 + 48) = 126$ g/dm³
Q4 a) $0.1 \times (20 \div 1000) = 0.002$ moles
b) **$2HCl + Ca(OH)_2$** $\rightarrow CaCl_2 + 2H_2O$
c) From the equation, **2** mole(s) of HCl reacts with **1** mole(s) of $Ca(OH)_2$
d) $0.002 \div 2 = 0.001$ moles
e) $0.001 \div (50 \div 1000) = 0.02$ mol/dm³
f) Concentration $= 0.02 \times (40 + 32 + 2) = 1.48$ g/dm³
Q5 a) Moles KOH $= 0.1 \times (30 \div 1000) = 0.003$
Reaction equation: $2KOH + H_2SO_4 \rightarrow K_2SO_4 + 2H_2O$, so $0.003 \div 2 = 0.0015$ moles of H_2SO_4.
concentration $= 0.0015 \div (10 \div 1000)$
$= 0.15$ mol/dm³
b) Mass in grams $= 0.15 \times (2 + 32 + 64) = 14.7$ g/dm³

Pages 115-116 — Water

Q1 a) air rises, water condenses — B
water flows — D
evaporation — A
rain — C
b) A
c) D

Q2 a)

SALT	SOLUBLE	INSOLUBLE
sodium sulfate	✓	
ammonium chloride	✓	
lead nitrate	✓	
silver chloride		✓
lead sulfate		✓
potassium chloride	✓	
barium sulfate		✓

b) i) Potassium chromate — soluble because all salts of potassium are soluble.
   ii) Vanadium nitrate — soluble because all nitrates are soluble.
Q3 pure, sulfur, power stations, acid, fertilisers, rocks, households
Q4 The following statements should be ticked:
Water is essential for life because many biological reactions take place in solution.
Fertilisers are often ammonium salts which are soluble in water.
Many covalent compounds like wax and petrol don't dissolve in water.

Chemistry 3(i) — Chemical Concepts

Q5 a)

negative charge → O H
H ← positive charge

b) i)

part of an NaCl crystal
(Na⁺ Cl⁻ Na⁺ / Cl⁻ Na⁺ Cl⁻ / Na⁺ Cl⁻ Na⁺)

ii) Ionic bonds / the attraction of the opposite charges / electrostatic forces of attraction.

iii) Diagram should look similar to:

dissolved sodium and chloride ions

Pages 117-118 — Solubility

Q1 solvent — a liquid which dissolves a solute.
solute — a substance which dissolves in a liquid.
solution — the mixture formed when a solute dissolves in a solvent.
saturated — a solution in which no more solute will dissolve.

Q2 a) grams per 100 grams of solvent
b) some solute remains undissolved
c) low, high

Q3 aquatic, oxygen, chlorine, bleach, carbon dioxide, pressure, fizzy

Q4 a)

mass of KCl used (g)	solubility (g / 100 g)	temperature (°C)
17	34	6
18	36	14
20	40	29
21	42	51
23	46	52

b), c) i) and d)

[graph of solubility vs temperature]

c) ii) Ami could repeat the experiment with this amount of potassium chloride to see if she gets a different result.

e) i) Accept an answer between 37 g / 100 g water and 38 g / 100 g water.
ii) 43 g / 100 g water (accept 42.5 – 43.5 g / 100 g water)

Q5 a) 55 g / 100 g
b) 105 g / 100 g (accept any answer between 103 and 105 g / 100 g)
c) i) lead nitrate
ii) potassium nitrate
d) 85 – 38 = 47 g / 100 g water (accept any answer between 45 and 50 g / 100 g)

Pages 119-120 — Hard Water

Q1 a) true
b) false
c) false
d) false
e) true

Q2 a) Tap water might already contain dissolved ions, which could affect the results.
b) i) magnesium sulfate and calcium chloride
ii) Because more soap was needed to produce a lather with these compounds/a scum was formed.
c) The distilled water sample acted as the control.
d) It works well in both hard and soft water and won't form a scum.

Q3 a) The kettle becomes less efficient / takes longer to boil.
b) E.g. any two of: Calcium ions are good for healthy bones and teeth. Scale inside pipes helps to prevent rust. Scale inside pipes may form a protective coating which helps to prevent poisonous metal ions getting into drinking water.

Q4 Na$_2$Resin(s) + Ca^{2+}(aq) → CaResin(s) + 2Na$^+$(aq) /
Na$_2$Resin(s) + Mg^{2+}(aq) → MgResin(s) + 2Na$^+$(aq)
The resin has sodium ions attached to it. It exchanges these for the Ca^{2+} and Mg^{2+} ions that make the water hard, removing them from the water.

Q5 a) Calcium carbonate isn't soluble in water, so there were no Ca^{2+} ions in solution.
b) i) CO$_2$(g) + H$_2$O(l) + CaCO$_3$(s) → **Ca(HCO$_3$)$_2$(aq)**
ii) The Ca(HCO$_3$)$_2$ is soluble in water, so there are now calcium ions in solution.
c) i) calcium carbonate (also accept 'scale')
ii) The calcium carbonate forms an insoluble deposit ('scale') which can reduce the efficiency of the heating system. It can eventually block the pipes altogether.
d) Using an acid — calcium carbonate dissolves in acid.

Page 121 — Water Quality

Q1 a) distilled water
b) chlorine taste

Q2 filtration — solids
chlorination — harmful microorganisms
adding iron compounds — phosphates
adding lime (calcium hydroxide) — acidity

Q3 a) B
b) D
c) A
d) C

Chemistry 3(ii) — Energy & Chemical Tests

Q4 a) It's too expensive, and people often live in isolated rural areas where the nearest source of water is a long distance away / the countries don't have the infrastructure to supply clean water.
b) The biggest increases in life expectancy have been related to the ability of countries to supply clean water.
Q5 a) They are poisonous.
b) bacteria / chemicals
c) by filtration (using gravel beds)

Pages 122-124 — Mixed Questions — Chemistry 3(i)

Q1 a) Atomic mass
b) He left gaps for undiscovered elements.
c) Group I
d) Group II
e) Group VII
f)

Period	Group I	Group II	Group III	Group VII	Group 0
2	Li 2,1	Be 2,2	B 2,3	F 2,7	Ne 2,8
3	Na 2,8,1	Mg 2,8,2	Al 2,8,3	Cl 2,8,7	Ar 2,8,8

Q2 a) The following should be underlined: ammonium nitrate, carbon dioxide, magnesium sulfate.
b) Magnesium sulfate
c) The solubility of a substance in a given solvent is the number of grams of the solute that dissolves in 100 g of the solvent at a particular temperature.
d) i) about 350 g
  ii) 350 − 190 = 160 g (allow answers between 150 g and 170 g)
e) Nitrates are removed using bacteria / microorganisms.
Q3 a) Decrease
b) Cl_2 (aq) + 2KBr (aq) → Br_2 (aq) + 2KCl (aq)
c) The green solution would turn brown.
d) Bromine is less reactive than chlorine, so it doesn't displace it from the solution.
Q4 a) Acids **release** H^+ ions — they are proton **donors**. Bases **accept** H^+ ions — they are proton **acceptors**.
b) It ionises almost completely in water / (nearly) every hydrogen atom is released to become a hydrated proton.
c) i) HCl
  ii) HCOOH
Q5 a) e.g. methyl orange
b) i) Moles NaOH = 0.5 × (20 ÷ 1000) = 0.01 moles
NaOH + HCl → NaCl + H_2O, so there's also 0.01 moles of HCl.
Concentration of HCl = 0.01 ÷ (25 ÷ 1000) = 0.4 mol/dm³
  ii) M_r HCl = 1 + 35.5. = 36.5
In 1 dm³: mass in grams = moles × M_r = 0.4 × 36.5 = 14.6 g/dm³
Q6 a) F, because it has a high melting point, a high density and it is a good conductor of electricity.
b) i) It is used as a catalyst (transition metals often make good catalysts).
  ii) Iron is very hard and strong, which makes it a good structural material.

Q7 a) i) D
  ii) E
  iii) D
  iv) E
b) ionic, water, hydrogen, hydroxide, gas, Hydrogen, a lighted splint
c) Their reactivity increases down the group. Group I elements lose an electron when they react. As you go down the group the electron in the outermost shell gets further away and more shielded from the attraction of the nucleus. This means it's more easily lost.

Chemistry 3(ii) — Energy & Chemical Tests

Page 125 — Energy

Q1 energy, exothermic, heat, an increase, endothermic, heat, a decrease
Q2 a) 29.5 °C − 22 °C = **7.5 °C** (accept 7 °C)
b) neutralisation, exothermic
c) Some energy is always lost to or gained from the surroundings.
Q3 a) photosynthesis
b) neutralisation
c) endothermic
d) exothermic
Q4 a) exothermic
b) A–C, because more energy is released when this bond forms than is taken in when the A–B bond is broken.

Page 126 — Energy and Fuels

Q1 a) exothermic
b) Because copper is such a good conductor of heat / because it is relatively unreactive.
c) Because heat energy is lost, e.g. in heating the can and the surrounding air.
Q2 a) Energy gain = 4.2 × 50 × 30.5 = 6405 J
b) Energy per gram = 6405 ÷ 0.7 = 9150 J/g = 9.15 kJ/g
Q3 a) Energy gain = 4.2 × 50 × 27 = 5670 J
Energy produced per gram = 5670 ÷ 0.8 = 7087.5 J/g = 7.09 kJ/g
b) Petrol would make the better fuel because it releases more energy per gram of fuel than fuel X does.
Q4 a) carbon dioxide / CO_2
b) Global warming / climate change / melting polar ice caps / rising sea levels / flooding / more hurricanes (other answers are possible)
c) Any 3 of: solar power, wind power, hydroelectric power, tidal power, geothermal power, biomass, wave power.
d) E.g. oil is non-renewable, so it's becoming rarer. As it becomes more rare it becomes more expensive, and so does everything transported by lorry, train or plane.

Chemistry 3(ii) — Energy & Chemical Tests

Pages 127-128 — Bond Energies

Q1 a) A, C and D
  b) B
  c) B and E
  d) D
Q2 a) the energy change / the enthalpy change
  b) endothermic
  c) exothermic
  d) The energy that is initially needed to break the bonds in the reactants.
  e) They usually speed up chemical reactions by lowering the activation energy.
Q3 a) ΔH = −90 kJ/mol.
  b) Activation energy = +70 kJ/mol.
  c) Activation energy = 90 + 70 = +160 kJ/mol.
Q4 a) (4 × 412) + (2 × 498) = 2644 kJ/mol.
  b) (2 × 743) + (4 × 463) = 3338 kJ/mol.
  c) ΔH = 2644 − 3338 = −694 kJ/mol.
Q5 ΔH = [158 + (4 × 391) + 498] − [945 + (4 × 463)] = −577 kJ/mol.
Q6 a) ΔH = [(2 × 348) + (12 × 412) + (7 × 498)] − [(8 × 743) + (12 × 463)] = −2374 kJ/mol.
  b) ΔH = −2374 ÷ 2 = −1187 kJ/mol.

Page 129 — Energy and Food

Q1 chemical, respiration, fat
Q2 a) The excess energy is stored as fat.
  b) A diet that provides the body with slightly less energy than it needs each day in order to lose weight.
Q3 a) eggs
  b) (331 ÷ 100) × 30 = 99.3 kcal.
Q4 a) 1 g of water, 1 °C, 4.2
  b) A Calorie actually means a kilocalorie, i.e. 1000 calories (or the amount of energy needed to raise the temperature of 1 kg of water by 1 °C).
  c) 270 × 4.2 = 1134 kJ.
Q5 glucose + **oxygen** → **carbon dioxide** + **water** + ENERGY

Pages 130-131 — Tests for Cations

Q1 Cations are positive ions. The prefix 'cat' is used because they're attracted to the cathode (the negative electrode).
Q2 a) brick-red flame — Ca^{2+}
  yellow-orange flame — Na^+
  crimson flame — Li^+
  yellow-green flame — Ba^{2+}
  lilac flame — K^+
  b) potassium nitrate
Q3 a)

Metal Cation	Colour of Precipitate
Fe^{2+}	green
Cu^{2+}	blue
Fe^{3+}	reddish brown
Al^{3+}	white

  b) Fe^{2+}**(aq)** + **2** OH^-(aq) → **Fe(OH)**$_2$**(s)**
  c) Fe^{3+}(aq) + $3OH^-$(aq) → Fe(OH)$_3$(s)
  d) A white precipitate forms that then dissolves in excess NaOH to form a colourless solution.

Q4 a) NH_4^+
  b) ammonia, NH_3
  c) Use damp red litmus paper — ammonia turns it blue.
  d) NH_4^+(aq) + OH^-(aq) → NH_3(g) + H_2O(l).
Q5 a) $CuSO_4$
  b) LiCl
  c) $Al_2(SO_4)_3$
  d) $FeSO_4$
  e) $FeCl_3$
  f) NH_4Cl
  g) $CaCl_2$

Page 132 — Tests for Anions

Q1 a) SO_4^{2-}
  b) I^-
  c) CO_3^{2-}
  d) NO_3^-
Q2 acid, carbon dioxide, limewater, colour, black, white
Q3 a) dilute hydrochloric acid, barium chloride solution
  b) a white precipitate (of barium sulfate)
  c) aluminium powder, sodium hydroxide solution
Q4 She could add dilute nitric acid to a solution of the compound, and then add some silver nitrate solution. If the compound contains Cl^- ions a white precipitate will form. If it contains Br^- ions a cream precipitate will form and if it contains I^- ions a yellow precipitate will form.
Q5 a) Ag^+(aq) + Cl^-(aq) → AgCl(s)
  b) 2HCl(aq) + Na_2CO_3(s) → 2NaCl(aq) + H_2O(l) + **CO_2(g)**
  c) **Ba^{2+}(aq) + SO_4^{2-}(aq)** → **$BaSO_4$(s)**
  d) $CuCO_3$(s) → **CuO(s) + CO_2(g)**

Pages 133-134 — Tests for Organic Compounds

Q1 a) yellowy-orange and/or blue
  b) Octane will be smokier. It has a higher proportion of carbon.
Q2 a) i) The volume of organic compound used, the volume of bromine water used, the time for which each sample is shaken.
    ii) To make it a fair test.
  b) B
  c) A
  d) The last two.
Q3 a) carbon dioxide and water
  b) ethene + **oxygen** → **carbon dioxide** + **water**
     C_2H_4 + $3O_2$ → $2CO_2$ + $2H_2O$
  c) carbon monoxide and carbon / soot
Q4 a) (12 ÷ 44) × 8.8 = 2.4 g of carbon
  b) (2 ÷ 18) × 5.4 = 0.6 g of hydrogen
  c) moles of C = 2.4 ÷ 12 = 0.2 mol
     moles of H = 0.6 ÷ 1 = 0.6 mol
  d) 0.2 : 0.6 = (0.2 ÷ 0.2) : (0.6 ÷ 0.2) = 1 : 3 ratio
     empirical formula is **CH_3**
Q5 a) mass of C = (12 ÷ 44) × 4.4 = 1.2 g
     mass of H = (2 ÷ 18) × 1.8 = 0.2 g
     moles of C = 1.2 ÷ 12 = 0.1 mol
     moles of H = 0.2 ÷ 1 = 0.2 mol
     ratio = 0.1 : 0.2 = (0.1 ÷ 0.1) : (0.2 ÷ 0.1) = 1 : 2
     empirical formula = **CH_2**

Chemistry 3(ii) — Energy & Chemical Tests

b) mass of C = (12 ÷ 44) × 1.1 = 0.3 g
mass of H = (2 ÷ 18) × 0.9 = 0.1 g
mass of O = 0.8 − 0.3 − 0.1 = 0.4 g
moles of C = 0.3 ÷ 12 = 0.025 mol
moles of H = 0.1 ÷ 1 = 0.1 mol
moles of O = 0.4 ÷ 16 = 0.025 mol
ratio = 0.025 : 0.1 : 0.025 = 1 : 4 : 1
empirical formula = **CH$_4$O**

Page 135 — Instrumental Methods

Q1 a) They are much faster than lab methods.
b) Any 2 of: They are more accurate than lab methods / They are sensitive, and can be used even with a very small sample / They don't need trained chemists to carry out the tests / The tests can be automated.
Q2 a) lithium, Li
b) E.g. the steel industry.
Q3 a) chromium, manganese and iron
b) C$_5$H$_{10}$
c) Antimony has two isotopes, one with an atomic mass M$_r$ of 121, and one with an atomic mass M$_r$ of 123.
Q4 a) nuclear magnetic resonance
b) organic compounds
c) hydrogen atoms

Pages 136-137 — Identifying Unknown Substances

Q1 Atomic absorption spectroscopy, mass spectrometry
Q2 a) Potassium, K$^+$, because it gives a lilac flame.
b) Iodide, I$^-$, because it gives a yellow precipitate in the final test.
c) Compound Y is ammonium sulfate, (NH$_4$)$_2$SO$_4$.
Q3 To test for iron(III) ions, dissolve some of the solid in water and add a few drops of NaOH solution. A reddish brown precipitate indicates iron(III).
To test for nitrate ions, mix a separate sample of the solid with a little aluminium powder, then add a few drops of NaOH solution. On heating, a gas should be released which can be tested with damp red litmus paper. The litmus paper turning blue indicates nitrate ions.
Q4 a) Ethanol. [M$_r$ = (2 × 12) + (6 × 1) + (1 × 16) = 46].
b) Nuclear magnetic resonance spectroscopy / infrared spectrometry / UV spectroscopy / gas-liquid chromatography.
Q5 a) Mass of C = (12 ÷ 44) × 1.37 = 0.37 g
Mass of H = (2 ÷ 18) × 1.12 = 0.12 g
Mass of O = 1 − 0.37 − 0.12 = 0.50 g
Moles of C = 0.37 ÷ 12 = 0.03 mol
Moles of H = 0.12 ÷ 1 = 0.12 mol
Moles of O = 0.50 ÷ 16 = 0.03 mol
Ratio = 0.03 : 0.12 : 0.003 = 1 : 4 : 1
Empirical formula = **CH$_4$O**.
b) Mass of CH$_4$O = 12 + 4 + 16 = 32.
Molecular formula is the same as the empirical formula, **CH$_4$O**.
c)
```
      H
      |
  H − C − O − H
      |
      H
```

Pages 138-140 — Mixed Questions — Chemistry 3(ii)

Q1 a) An exothermic reaction. It gives out energy to the surroundings.
b) less than
c) e.g. you could use calorimetry, where the food or fuel is burnt and the energy from the flame is used to heat up a certain amount of water in a copper container. The change in the temperature of the water can be used to work out the amount of energy released by the substance.
d) Energy gain = 4.2 × 100 × 15 = 6300 J
Energy produced per gram = 6300 ÷ 0.5 = 12 600 J/g = 12.6 kJ/g
Q2 a) He would see a sludgy green precipitate.
b) That the compound contains copper(II) / Cu^{2+} ions.
c) Cu^{2+}(aq) + 2OH$^-$(aq) → Cu(OH)$_2$(s)
d) He could add dilute hydrochloric acid / HCl to the compound, followed by barium chloride / BaCl$_2$ and look for a precipitate.
e) CuSO$_4$
Q3 a) 2000 × 4.2 = 8400 kJ
b) The woman is getting 400 kJ of energy less than she needs each day, so she will gradually lose weight.

Q4 a)

[Graph showing energy vs progress of reaction with two curves A and B, reactants higher than products, ΔH marked]

b) B
c) exothermic
d) i) N$_2$ + 3H$_2$ → 2NH$_3$
ii) [945 + (3 × 436)] − [6 × 391] = −93 kJ/mol
iii) The reaction in which ammonia is formed. The diagram shows an exothermic reaction. The reaction in which ammonia is formed is also exothermic (it has a negative ΔH), but the reaction in which HI is formed is endothermic (it has a positive ΔH).
Q5 a) Moles of C = 240 ÷ 12 = 20
Moles of O = 160 ÷ 16 = 10
Moles of H = 60 ÷ 1 = 60
Ratio = 20 : 10 : 60 = 2 : 1 : 6
Empirical formula = C$_2$H$_6$O.
b) There are only single bonds between the carbons / there are no double or triple bonds between carbons / the compound is saturated.
Q6 a) ammonia
b) Ag$^+$(aq) + Cl$^-$(aq) → AgCl(s)
c) ammonium chloride
Q7 a) E.g. atomic absorption spectroscopy / IR spectrometry / UV spectroscopy / NMR spectroscopy / gas-liquid chromatography / mass spectrometry.
b) E.g. medical tests / police forensic work / environmental analysis / drugs testing / analysis of industrial materials.
c) More accurate instruments can be produced more cheaply. Instrumental methods can perform a more detailed analysis more quickly, and with more accurate results.
Q8 a) Ca^{2+}
b) CO$_3^{2-}$ (or HCO$_3^-$)
c) Fe^{3+}
d) SO$_4^{2-}$